SPATIAL ASPECTS OF SETTLEMENT PATTERNS

SPATIAL ASPECTS OF SETTLEMENT PATTERNS

A Study of the Narmada Command Area of Mahesana District, Gujarat

ANJANA P. DESAI

Foreword by

A.B. MUKERJI

CONCEPT PUBLISHING COMPANY, NEW DELHI

Research report of study sponsored by the Narmada Planning Group, Irrigation Department, Government of Gujarat.

First Published 1985

Published by

Naurang Rai
Concept Publishing Company
H-13, Bali Nagar
NEW DELHI-110015 (India)

Printed in India by

Hans Raj Gupta & Sons
Anand Parbat
NEW DELHI-110005

Foreword

Books on settlement geography written by Indian geographers on Indian areas are numerous and the approaches adopted in them are diverse, but a majority of them lack a consistent conceptual perspective that reflects the growth of an indigenous school of thinking or an adaptation of the western mode of analysis to Indian spatial and landscape reality. Many books have dealt entirely with rural settlements while urban settlements develop as the prime focus of urban geography. In the taxonomy of human geography settlement geography is undoubtedly a first-order branch while rural settlement geography and urban geography are second order branches. On this logical premise there is a legitimate case for the study of the parents (settlement geography which is an integration of the two geographies, rural and urban settlement) and the offspring, rural settlement geography and urban geography. Unfortunately, there is no appropriate abbreviation for rural settlements, for, rural in rural settlement geography is not the same as rural in common parlance and is therefore entirely different from rural geography which etymologically should mean an umbrella concept, much more inclusive. Surely, one approach to overcome the difficulty in completely understanding the character of the settlement fabric in an area would be to ignore the distinction, howsoever valid this might be both in logic and empirical reality, and to integrate the two components, rather merge them, and thus treat the settlements per se and not as urban or rural settlements. The outcome of this mode of analysis is the admirable book written by Dr. Anjana Desai.

Financed by the Narmada Planning Group, the book, for obvious reasons is heavily oriented toward the empirical parameters of the settlement system of a part of Mahesana district of Gujarat which is located in the Narmada Command Area. There is an altogether marked departure from the Sauerian Cultural-Landscape or the Chicago School Pattern-Functionalist approach. Dr. Desai's major concern is to understand those pattern-properties which are of immediate relevance to policy formulations for regional development, and not to discover the origin and evolution of the system on the one hand and the future trends on the other. Unconstrained by the practically convenient but theoretically and empirically unsound Census of India definitions, Dr. Desai attempts to classify the hierarchy of settlements in an integrated spectrum on the twin bases of size and functions, both extremely important in all analytical discussions.

For policy formulations on the implementation of structural and infrastructural elements as an integral component of the unconditionally committed distributive justice goal of all development efforts the settlement system analysis is a *sine que non*. Dr. Desai has kept this theme in the foreground throughout her perceptive and penetrating study. In most of the extant studies settlements have been treated as individuals and generalisations have been derived therefrom, thus precluding the realisation of the opportunity of acquiring an understanding of those characteristics which are generated, sustained, and modified by the interactions. That settlement fabric is a valid concept had been well understood but that this fabric subsumes a system of interacting settlements needs to be emphasised. Dr. Desai has done that and more.

She has applied most of the widely used quantitative techniques in describing and analysing the parameters of the settlement fabric and system. Apart from yielding insights into the theme these discussions and techniques will most surely provide models and guidelines to similar studies focusing on other areas. In this aspect, the book will be greatly useful to the novitiates in geography and to practising settlement planners. It will equally well serve as a primer in applied quantitative geography with easily comprehensible examples fully worked out.

The net result of this comprehensive analysis is Dr. Desai's bold distinction between policy aims directed at 'people-prosperity' and 'place-prosperity', terms coined with telling connotations and suggesting what earlier have been referred to as spatial distributive justice distinguished from social distributive justice. The former has been derived from the mathematics of development potential, which is a conversion of qualitative attributes and concepts into quantitative measures.

The book does honour to the school of Indian settlement geographers by contributing significantly to the application of modern quantitative techniques, to the analytical tools and concepts, and to policy formulations. Settlement geographers will legitimately take pride in this commendable effort.

Professor of Geography
Punjab University
Chandigarh

A.B. MUKERJI

26 October 1984

Preface

THE subject of settlements is an age-old yet fascinating branch of human geography. The interplay of natural and human factors leads to an unending variety of settlement patterns. The unravelling of these factors—physiographic, climatic, cultural, socio-economic, behavioural and so on is necessary for perceiving some order in what might otherwise look like a random pattern on space. A framework based on such perception can be helpful in the planning process—for example while undertaking a major irrigation project.

The study presented here is an effort to understand the settlement system in six talukas of Mahesana District of northern Gujarat, which would be falling under the Narmada Command Area. This study area represents an interesting case of marked natural and human variability in a region of limited extent, which could be surveyed within a reasonable time.

Rainfall and soil salinity, two very important agro-climatic variables, show a distinct east-west gradient from the fringe of the Rann of Kutch to the eastern part around Kalol. But this is not the only factor in determining the distribution and the size of settlements. The survey revealed infrastructural differences—for example accessibility—and also cultural differences in people's attitude and socio-economic status. Census data of 1951, 1961, 1971 and 1981 were utilised in a simple gravity model of population potential to understand the growth of settlements. This analysis vividly brought out the mutual reinforcement effort of proximal settlements on each other; thus initially sparsely settled areas continue to remain so. Some indication of the prosperity brought by irrigation is also seen in the east for example in the intensity of cropping pattern.

With its emphasis on a close view of different types of settlements, the study ultimately tries to raise certain planning issues: should we try to further enhance existing growth centres, or should equitable resource distribution over space be our goal? How far should we emphasise physical resources as against human resources?

If this modest effort is found a useful source material by a few planners, geographers, social scientists and the like, it would have served its purpose.

Department of Geography
Gujarat University
Ahmedabad, India.

ANJANA P. DESAI

Autumn of 1984

Acknowledgements

IT GIVES me immense pleasure to acknowledge the opportunity and the financial aid that the members of the Narmada Planning Group (NPG), Gandhinagar gave me to study the settlement pattern both from the theoretical and empirical points of view. My special thanks are due to Dr. Y.K. Alagh, Dr. B.N. Vishwanath, Dr. S.R. Hashim, Shri B.J. Desai, Shri V.M. Patel and Shri P.B. Buch of the NPG. I am thankful to Dr. B.B. Patel of Sardar Patel Institute of Social and Economic Research, Ahmedabad, Dr. M.C. Jaiswal of the Department of Statistics and Dr. V.P. Shah, Head of the Sociology Department of Gujarat University and other university colleagues for lively academic discussions and concrete suggestions. Mr. R.S. Chhaya, Director of Census, Ahmedabad, has kindly provided me with all the volumes of the census for our work and Prof. V.G. Dalal helped in depicting the maps and diagrams through photographic lens. Shri P.M. Trivedi and Dr. Vinay Kamble have been a constant source of encouragement at times of despair. I wish to express my thanks to Shri Ambalal Upadhyaya who provided a guideline of Mahesana before commencement of the field work.

I am grateful to Prof. A.B. Mukerji, Head of the Geography Department of Punjab University, Chandigarh, for writing the Foreword to the book and to Concept Publishing Company who have generously offered to publish this research report.

I had the rewarding experience of working with a batch of very enthusiastic and intelligent research fellows who took up the challenge of working in an integrated fashion to complete the work in six months. My sincere thanks are due to them—Smt. Smita Sen Gupta, Smt. Mitali Sarkar, Smt. Radha Chauhan, Shri Shafee Contractor. Skilful and enthusiastic programming consultancy was provided by Shri Vishnubhai D. Thakkar. Kum. Damayanti Patel gave the magic touch of her cartographic skill to all maps and diagrams, while Smt. Harsha Shukla toiled over the accounts and secretarial work. Shri Dinesh Vaghela and Shri Daya Purabia gave me all attendance whenever I needed it. I am thankful to all Field Investigators who carried out the field survey in a very short time—they are Shri Vasudev S. Patel, Sanjay M. Vaishnav, Vijay R. Thakar, Abheysinh F. Dabhi, Dilip Parmar, Alajibhai H. Rathod, Rohit Pittaliya, Mahesh M. Parmar, Himansu H. Mehta, Prakash P. Sharma and Bharat M. Patel. I am also thankful to Shri Snehal Shah for providing me with excellent xerox copies. Shri Narayana has put in painstaking efforts to type the manuscript in a short time. I sincerely extend my thanks to all of them. Lastly, this work could not have been completed without the constant encouragement of my family, which should not be taken for granted.

ANJANA P. DESAI

Contents

List of Maps

List of Figures

List of Tables

1

INTRODUCTION

MEANING OF SETTLEMENT

HUMAN beings agglomerate themselves at a particular geographic location in the form of a settlement for work and living. Settlements develop in a combined environment of natural and man-made setting, having various types of houses, institutions and amenities, suited to the need of residents. Every settlement is unique—its growth and evolution depend on its evironment, availability of resources, technology at hand, cultural and social values of residents and its management system. It is a dynamic unit and has distinct characteristics reflected in its size, structural morphology, demographic and functional features, communication and network system of its own and socio-economic linkages with other settlements. Whether a settlement should be termed 'rural' or 'urban' depends on the decision of governments, of different countries, based on these factors. The growth or decline of settlements depends on the overall quality of human life, involving physical environment with social atmosphere, economic opportunity, housing, health and education facilities with other amenities of life.

SCOPE OF SETTLEMENT STUDY

Settlements form a pattern on space and can be expressed as a structure of points, lines and areas. Places of residence and work, centres of production may be considered as "points" around which human beings are organized. The network of communication are the "lines" of human interaction and "areas" are the zones of socio-economic linkages around a node as well as between nodes. Both the structure and interaction are dependent on each other and are constantly changing in a dynamic system. Thus a settlement needs to be analysed in a system over time and space.

The scope and relevance of the study of a settlement pattern lie in the question, why are spatial distribution structured the way they are? Why and how do they vary over time and space? Settlement structure reflects the way the production and distribution systems are organized, based on the resource and technology at a particular point of time. It is important to understand the process and the structure that have created such a system. Such knowledge of linkage between spatial process and spatial structure in settlement systems can help us manipulate or plan the spatial organization that we desire to have. The mobilization of resources or emphasis of growth can be monitored.

OBJECTIVES OF THIS STUDY

The objectives of this study of settlements are limited. The emphasis here has been laid on the demographic variables rather than on economic aspects. The main reason for this is the non-availability of published economic data at a village level. It is hoped that the direct or indirect impact of economic and non-economic factors can be inferred from the growth size, density, distribution and composition of population of settlements in this area. The growth of population is a complex phenomenon of interacting processes of physical, economic and technological developments. This study intends to analyse only some aspects of it for 546 villages (including six towns) in a limited period available for this study.

The main objectives of this study are as follows:

(a) to understand the spatial pattern of settlements in a rural setting, as the organization of settlements on space reflects the differential use and availability of resources;

(b) to analyse the demographic variables that have given rise to such a system or pattern of settlements;

(c) to know and analyse the various factors that are responsible for such a pattern of population in settlements;

(d) to understand the impact of irrigation on the growth of population of settlements; and

(e) to classify settlements in functional and demographic hierarchy and the overall development potentiality of settlements in the study area.

THE STUDY AREA

Locational aspects

The study area comprises six talukas (Sami, Harij, Chanasma, Mahesana, Kadi, Kalol) of Mahesana district of North Gujarat (Map. 1.1). The general information of the area by taluka is given in Table 1.1. Out of 11 talukas, these six talukas cover

TABLE 1.1: **Area and population of the study region by taluka**

Taluka	Area in km^2 1971	Population 1951	Population 1961	Population 1971	Estimated population 1981
Sami	1509.8	52398	71000	95858	128911
Harij	407.0	33655	44039	55161	68960
Chanasma	886.7	113837	140578	174284	216997
Mahesana	791.4	148578	186668	246212	395336
Kadi	829.7	123147	146913	182674	215910
Kalol	487.2	106441	129342	172533	191900
Total:	4911.8	578056	718540	928722	1218014

Source : *District Census Handbook*, 1951, 1961, 1971.

a total of 4911.8 km^2, that is, over 50 per cent of the total area of the district (9027 km^2). The study area extends from 71° 33′ E to 72° 55′ E and 23° 05′ N to 23° 52′ N, bordered by Radhanpur, Patan and Visnagar talukas in the north, Surendranagar district, Ahmedabad district in the south, Vijapur, Visnagar of Mahesana district and Gandhinagar district in the east, Little Rann of Kutch, and Ahmedabad district in the west. In the area, the relative situation or location is better for Mahesana and Kalol talukas as these are closer to the National Highway and the railway lines from

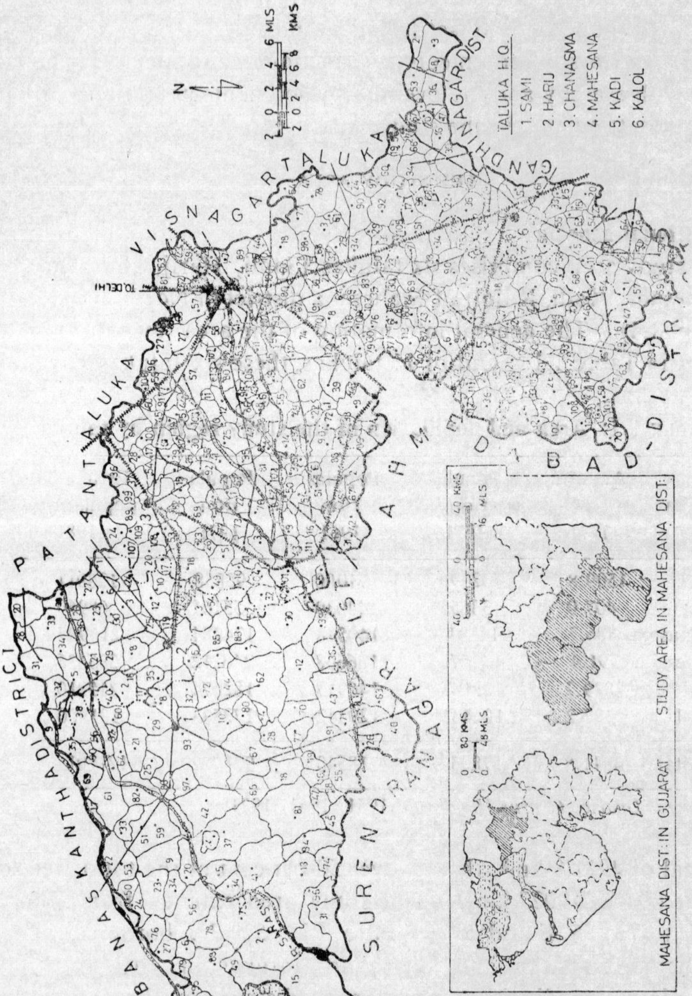

MAP 1.1: *Location map of the study area: Six talukas of Mahesana district*

Ahmedabad to Delhi and are closer to large urban centres like Ahmedabad and Gandhinagar.

Relevance of selection of this area

The study area comprises six of the 62 talukas in the command area of the Narmada River Project. The study area, especially Kalol Mahesana talukas, has enjoyed the benefit of underground water over a period of 20 years. The total irrigated area has increased from 58,550 hectares in 1961-1962 to 109,371 hectares in 1977-1978 in the study area.

It is expected that an increase in the availability of water has an impact on agriculture in terms of total production, other economic activities like agro-based industries and trading activities related to agricultural produce, development of infrastructure and amenities and eventually on the general economic health of settlements and their population. Of course, the factors responsible for the growth of population may not necessarily be economic oriented; other important factors of control are physical and cultural.

The relevance of studying settlements of this part of the Narmada Command Area lies in understanding the impact of irrigation along with other factors on various aspects of demography like growth rate, density, distribution and composition of population, and the findings of this study can be useful to other areas of the command area.

A brief historical background of the study area

The study area is the southern part of Mahesana district which was founded by Mahesaji during the Rajput period in the 12th or 13th century. During 1572 to 1723, the district was ruled by the Viceroys appointed by the Mughal Emperor. The Gaekwads of Baroda had the hold of the area till 1949, when Baroda was merged into Bombay state. On the bifurcation of Bombay on May 1, 1960, the Mahesana district was included in the state of Gujarat. During the time of former Baroda state, the headquarters of the district was Kadi, but later, in 1902, it was shifted to Mahesana.

The Mahesana district, as it exists today, has undergone several territorial changes, internal and external. The external changes were caused due to transfer of areas to adjacent districts and internal changes were consequential and administrative. These changes may be broadly classified as under:

1. The integration of States and Estates in 1949;
2. The internal restructuring of the district in 1952;
3. The reconstitution of the district on account of transfer of Radhanpur and Santalpur talukas to the Banaskantha district in 1958;
4. The reduction of "Prants" from 3 to 2 in 1963;
5. The transfer of 25 villages of Kalol taluka to the Gandhinagar district in 1964; and
6. The conversion of the Harij Mahal into a taluka in 1966.

A brief outline of physical features

Relief

The general slope of the land is from north-east to south-west. By and large the area is a flat one, except for few hillocks around Kalol, Kadi and south-east of Mahesana.

River system

The entire areas is drained by four rivers—the Sabarmati, Rupen, Saraswati and Banas—following the general slope of the land. River Sabarmati is the only perennial river which flows through Kalol taluka. River Rupen flows through Mahesana, Chanasma and Sami talukas and disappears into the Little Rann of Kutch. River Banas and Saraswati pass through Harij and Sami talukas. The rivers get flooded during the rainy season and get choked in their load.

Climatic conditions

The average annual rainfall increases from west (45 cm) to east (75 cm) and the mean maximum temperature is 42°C and minimum is 7.5°C. The distribution of rainfall is erratic and the State Committee has classified Sami and Harij talukas as chronically drought-prone areas.

Soil

The main soil forming rocks are sandstone, shale, granite and conglomerates. Sami and Harij talukas are covered with Sami type, Kathiwada, Tarora and Koddha series. Sami type is sandy in nature with high permeability. Kathiwada varies between clay loam and sandy loam, Tarora is of clayey type, whereas Koddha series of Sami and Harij is highly saline and alkaline in nature and is not suitable for cultivation. Soils of Chanasma and Mahesana are sandy loam suited to the cultivation of cereals, pulses, cotton and spices. Both Kadi and Kalol have sandy and black clayey soils. Sami and Harij talukas experience dust-storms during April-May. The problem is created with wind-blown sand particles being deposited from the Rann, making the quality of soils poorer for cultivation. Salt pans are quite common in this side.

Vegetation

The vegetation cover is thicker with taller deciduous trees in Mahesana, Kalol and Kadi talukas while it is of xerophytic type with thorny leaves, deep roots and is stunted in size in the western parts of Sami and Harij talukas.

Ground water resource

Two major aquifers have been identified in the area. The depth of the aquifer A is 5 to 10 metres, but it is more than 20 metres, for aquifer B. The quality of the ground water deteriorates from the north-east to the south-west in the Sami area. Due to excessive exploitation, the level of the water table of A and B has declined 20 m during 1960—1975.

2

CONCEPTUAL FRAMEWORK, METHODOLOGY AND DATA ASPECTS

CONCEPTUAL FRAMEWORK

THIS study has been designed, first, to explain the pattern of settlements on space (Fig. 2.1) with various models and statistical techniques. Secondly, demographic variables have been examined, in terms of distribution, density, growth rate, size and composition of population. Thirdly, factors related to the growth or decline of population of settlements have been analysed. These are physical factors, irrigation, along with land use and crop pattern, impact of location and connectivity, functional or occupational pattern, aspects of infrastructure and social amenities. Finally, settlements have been classified by functional and population hierarchy and by development potentials. Various tables, both univariate and bivariate type, simple and composite graphs, maps of distribution, flow-map, isometric type, residual maps, computer mapping of dynamic population potential models, statistical testing, correlation analysis and chi-square tests have been used wherever it was necessary.

METHODOLOGY REGARDING THE PATTERN

The spatial pattern of settlements in terms of distribution, degree of dispersion and concentration has been measured in the following manner:

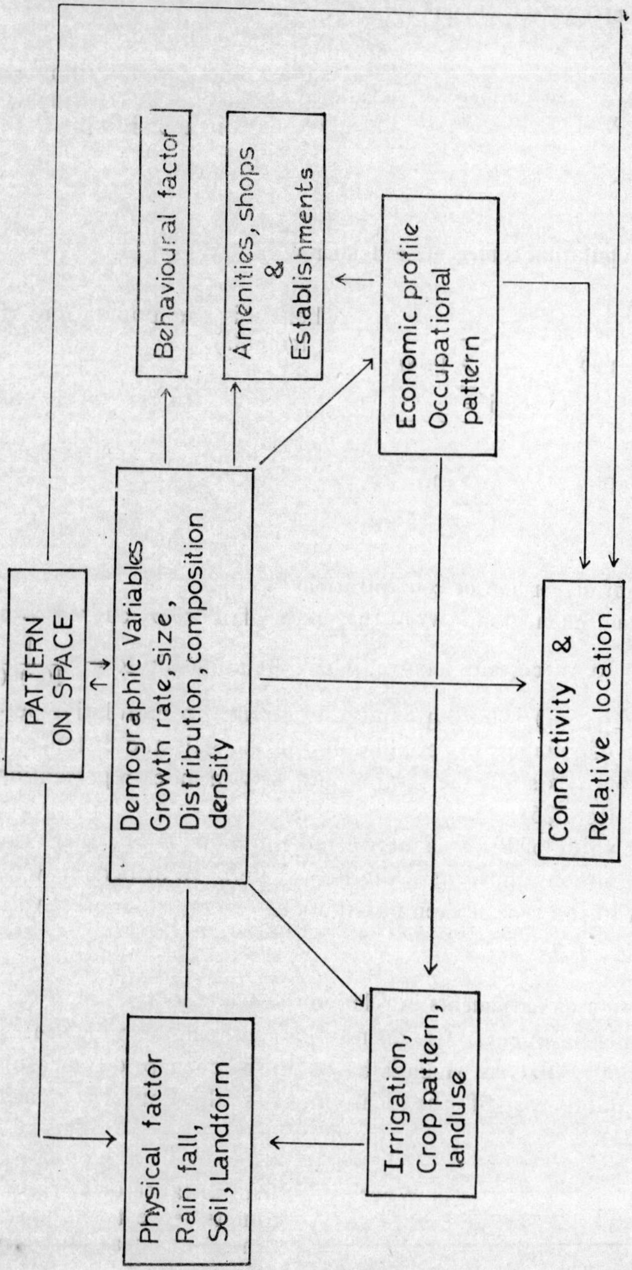

FIG. 2.1: *A schematic diagram of settlement study*

Mean centre of settlements

$$\frac{\sum_{i=1}^{n} x_i}{N} \; ; \; \frac{\sum_{i=1}^{n} y_i}{N}$$

(using x and y as co-ordinates of location of all settlements by linear distance in km)

Mean population centre of settlements

$$\frac{\sum_{i=1}^{n} p_i x_i}{\sum_{i=1}^{n} p_i} \; ; \; \frac{\sum_{i=1}^{n} p_i y_i}{\sum_{i=1}^{n} p_i}$$

(where p is the population of settlements)

Degree of dispersion or concentration

This has been done with the help of Lorenz curve with respect to a certain centre, where relationship $R = \frac{1}{10{,}000}$ $(p_{k-1} q_k - q_{k-1} p_k)$ where p and q represent the cumulative percentage of villages or population in one axis and distance in the other axis of the graph and k is an index representing points (Ref. 25).

The value of R varies between 0 and 1, if R=0, then the distribution is uniform, while R=1 refers to dispersion with respect to the line of even distribution, which is denoted with an angle of 45°.

Dispersion of settlements in relation to each other

This measurement has been done with the help of Nearest Neighbour Analysis which is based on the concept of measuring randomness of the location of settlements on space: (Ref. 21).

$$\bar{D}_{ran} = \frac{1}{2\sqrt{\frac{N}{A}}}$$

Where $\bar{D}$ = mean distance of a centre from its nearest neighbour (centre) in linear distance of km.

N = No. of centres

A = Area under consideration (taluka)

$$R = \frac{\bar{D}_{obs}}{1 \div \left(2\sqrt{\frac{N}{A}}\right)} \quad \text{where } R = \frac{\text{Measured Mean Distance}}{\text{Expected Mean Distance}}$$

$$R = 2\,\bar{D}_{obs}\sqrt{\frac{(N)}{A}}$$

where R varies between 0 (clustering) to 2.15 (uniform) and R=1 suggests random distribution

Comparison between observed and expected number of settlements and population

Chi-square tests have been used to compare the actual and expected number of settlements and total population by taluka in terms of area in the following manner:

$$\underset{\text{(Chi-square)}}{\kappa^2} = \sum_{i=1}^{n} \frac{(\text{obs} - \text{Exp})^2}{\text{Exp}}$$

Population potential

Potential of each settlement is an aggregate measure of the influence of the sum of population of its own and sum of population of other places, divided by its respective distances from them. In other words, it measures the potentiality of a centre to grow due to the presence of other centres around it, which provides the basis of socio-economic interactions (Ref. 1.21).

This exercise has been used in a dynamic way by changing the data to analyse the changes of population potential surfaces over three decades (1951-1981), with the help of computer mapping. An isometric map of population potential brings out clearly the three-dimensional effect of the potential surfaces of proportionate height. Cross-sections have also been added to bring out the same effect. The population potential model is as follows:

$$p_i(Ex) = \sum_{\substack{j=1 \\ j \neq i}}^{n} \frac{M_j}{d_{ij}}$$

where p_i Ex = Population potential of i, exclusive of centre

M_j = Population of j

d_{ij} = Distance between i and j, measured in km as co-ordinates from taluka headquarters

$$p_i(IN) = p_i(Ex) + \frac{M_i}{D_1}$$

where p_i (IN) = Population potential of i, inclusive of centre

$d_i = \frac{1}{2}$ of nearest neighbour distance from centre i.

High population potential values indicate that villages are large in size, closely spaced, and more in number; low values suggest the reverse of it.

Rank-size rule

In order to understand the existence of distortions in the hierarchical structure within the system of settlements, rank size rule has been used. Arranging a set of settlements, ranked in descending order of population size, the rank-size rule establishes a relationship such that, the population of the nth settlement is $1/n^{th}$ the size of the largest settlement's population, p_1;

$$p_n = \frac{p_1}{n}$$

The rank-size rule helps in comparing the actual hierarchical system of settlements with that of the expected one, on a logarithmic scale, by referring to a 1/n line with a slope of —1. The exercise has been repeated over time and space to know whether the hierarchical system has changed and how it differs from an irrigated area to that of an unirrigated area.

METHODOLOGY REGARDING DEMOGRAPHIC VARIABLES

Distribution

This aspect of population has been analysed with dot and

circle maps over time (1951 and 1981) and space. The change in the pattern has been graphically studied for two talukas—one with irrigation and higher rainfall (Kalol) and the other without irrigation and low rainfall (Sami) to note the variation of distribution of population over space.

Density

With the help of mapping, density of population has been analysed over time. Density of population has been analysed also in relation to population potential with the help of a residual map. An attempt has been made to know the association between the average distribution of rainfall of 30 years and density of population on space.

Growth rate

Growth rate of population has been analysed by decade with the help of a series of maps. The nature of growth has been combined for three decades as indicated in the sampling technique. Growth rates have been analysed in terms of taluka, whole study area and of the district. Growth rates of settlements have been ranked by taluka as well as by study area and are divided into four quartiles to denote as Q_1, Q_2, Q_3, Q_4 as low, average, moderate and high growth rates respectively.

Size of settlements

Settlements have been classified in a bivariate table for 1951 and 1981 and also in univariate distribution by decade on a composite graph. The distribution of size of settlements between an irrigated taluka (Kalol) and an unirrigated taluka (Sami) has been analysed.

Composition

Literacy, sex ratio and work-participation have been studied over space to know the quality of population. Age-structure is not done as it is not available on a village level.

METHODOLOGY FOR THE FACTORS PERTAINING TO THE GROWTH OR DECLINE OF SETTLEMENTS

The impact of physical factors like rainfall, soil and salinity has been examined with the help of regression analysis or by mapping. Correlation analysis and bivariate tables with Chi-square tasting have been made to understand whether aspects of occupational pattern (e.g. non-primary workers, per cent of female workers) have any relationship with demographic variables like size, density or growth-rate. Similarly, statistical techniques have been used to note the relationship between growth and decline of villages with types of amenities, and the number of shops and establishments. Weightages have been allotted to the type of amenities by the method of scarcity, that is, the higher the weightage the more scarce it is in existence. Thirty amenities have been aggregated from the census by village, including education and medical facilities, drinking water, electricity, post and telegraph, road and bus services. A list of weightage for amenities is given in Appendix II. A map of relative location has been prepared with the help of aggregating distance of a village from the district headquarters, taluka headquarters, from the nearest town, from the railway station. Distance has been measured by co-ordinates of villages, for avoiding the problem of selection of roads to have minimum distance.

Weightage has been given in terms of distance to its reference point, e.g. taluka headquarters, etc. The higher the net distance from these specific points of a village, the lower is the weightage given to that village for relative location. An isopleth map has been drawn based on the information of relative location. Similarly, connectivity has been shown in another isopleth map with villages having an aggregate score on the type of roads (metalled or unmetalled) and type of bus services (whole year or fair weather). A flow map has been prepared from the frequency of buses to and fro from a village per day, to indicate the level of interaction in terms of passengers. (The source of the data is the information available at the State Transport bus station).

In these isopleth maps, the average value is calculated, then the central class defined to include values from average minus one-half of the average to average plus one-half of the average. Thus the range of this central class equals the average value. The next higher class, called moderate, has a range equal to half the average value. The extreme classes, low and high, have been kept without limits at one end. In some maps, where range is large by the above method, the central class is taken from average minus one-quarter average to average plus one-quarter average, giving it a range of one-half average. In such cases, five classes are made instead of four.

Location Quotient of non-primary workers has been used to know the share of non-primary workers to total workers of a taluka to that of the district as a whole. Triangular graph, depicting three types of occupation (primary, secondary and tertiary) has been used for sample villages to know the occupational pattern. Finally, villages have been classified by two methods:

(i) functional-cum-population hierarchy of villages with more than 2,000 population in 1971: A rank-correlation has been used to establish a relationship between the number of functions and size of settlements from the census data. A composite map of hierarchy of function and size has been made to note the match or mismatch between the two variables. Here frequency of functions cannot be included, only types of functions have been considered due to the non-availability of data. However, such an analysis has been attempted for the selected villages where the type and number of shops and establishments have been correlated with the size of population.

(ii) with the help of 14 major variables, e.g. population of 1981, growth rate of population (1971-81), density 1981, agro-density 1981, per cent of irrigated land to total cultivated land 1971, total cultivated land 1971, population potential 1981, per cent of workers 1971, per cent of non-primary workers 1971, amenities 1971 (of 30 types), connectivity 1971, bus services 1981, relative location 1971, per cent of female workers 1971 and per cent of female literacy 1971, villages have been classified into groups of Development Potential (1971-1981) to know the potentiality for villages to develop or grow. Some data of 1971 have been used as percentages, assuming that the figures will not vary in a glaring manner in percentages in 1981, as the detailed census reports are not yet published. This development potential by computer mapping helps in understanding the area which is favourable for both population and economic growth. A decision on short-term and long-term planning can be made accordingly.

DATA ASPECTS

This study has emphasized mainly the demographic aspect and indirectly the economic growth of settlements. This is mainly due to the non-availability of economic data at village level on income, total population, yield per acre, holdings of land, total annual revenue of the village, total savings of villagers, per cent of cash crops to food crops, per cent of sale of crops to total crops produced, bank-loan/defaulting rate, per cent of landless labour, and so on. There is also non-availability of data in the demographic aspect, on village level, e.g. birth and death rate, migration (both in and out) and distribution of population by age-group. As a result, this study has not attempted to relate growth rate, which is a function of migration and natural growth of birth over death, and economic health of a village. A detailed household survey can be helpful in this respect for future study. In this study, primary data was collected on the amenities and number of shops and establishments by village and not on household basis. Secondary data have been the major source, e.g. census for population, amenities, occupation data, soil salinity data by remote-sensing method from the Space Applications Centre, Ahmedabad, rainfall distribution map from the Indian Meteorological Department, Pune, and other sources from Government and private publications.

In many cases, data are not available in the census for two points of time, e.g. irrigated land or data on land use by village. Similarly crop pattern by village was not available consistently for a decade. A comparison of occupation pattern for two points of time was not possible as the definition of occupational groups has changed in the census in 1961, 1971 and 1981.

A detailed data on migration (origin and destination) and the causes of migration is essential for the study of the processes that are responsible for the growth and decline of villages. In this situation, this study puts an emphasis on population aspects rather than the economic health of villages, to arrive at certain conclusions.

DEVELOPMENT OF HYPOTHESES

The following hypotheses can be developed in this study:

(a) growth rate of population is inversely related to the size of the village;
(b) total population and density of population is positively related to the per cent of irrigated land, though growth rate has no relationship with it;
(c) growth rate is related inversely to the per cent of female literacy and achievement in the family planning programme;
(d) density of population is associated with the distribution of rainfall and salinity of soil;
(e) total population is positively related to connectivity and the relative location of villages;
(f) size of village and existence of amenities, shops and establishments are directly related; and
(g) density and size of population are related to the existence of non-agricultural employment in villages.

The above hypotheses have been tested both qualitatively and quantitatively to arrive at certain conclusions. The experience from field work has been very helpful to understand qualitatively the growth and decline of a village, both in demographic and economic terms. For instance, field experience brings out clearly non-measurable cultural and behavioural factors, of people, which may be responsible for demographic growth, especially in the Sami area.

SAMPLING TECHNIQUE

In order to have a close view of a few villages in terms of

their population growth and decline, out of a total of 546 settlements of the area, purposive sampling was carried out. The idea was to have a quick look at the functional characteristics, irrigation facilities, system of connectivity, infrastructure, existence of shops and establishments of few villages, and, if possible, to have some idea of economic linkages and migration pattern. Since the field work was based only on general observations and discussions on a village level and not on a household basis, an overall impression can only be inferred.

For the purpose of sampling, initially growth rates of all villages for three decades (1951-61, 1961-71, 1971-81) were calculated and then villages were grouped by quartiles of growth rates depicted as Q_1, Q_2, Q_3 and Q_4 by taluka in each decade. Then villages were classified by a combined growth rates of three decades into the following nine groups:

Group	*Combination of growth rate*
1. Constantly high	Villages mainly with Q_4 (quartile four) growth rate and one Q_3 (quartile three) in three decades.
2. Constantly low	Mostly Q_1 (quartile one) in all three decades.
3. Increasingly high	Constantly increasing growth rate, in three decades.
4. Decreasingly low	Constantly decreasing growth rates.
5. Fluctuating cases	With high (Q_3/Q_4), low (Q_1/Q_2) and high (Q_3/Q_4) growth rate or Low-High-Low growth combinations.
6. Sudden growth	Low rate of growth (Q_1/Q_2) in the first two decades then sudden high (Q_3/Q_4) in last decade.
7. Sudden fall	High growth rate (Q_4/Q_3) in the first two decades and then sudden fall (Q_1) in the growth rate in the last decade.
8. Average growth	Combination of quartiles 2 and 3.
9. Mixed growth	All combinations that are not covered by the above groups.

After classifying settlements by growth rates by three decades, a bivariate table of population size groups was prepared for the year 1951 and 1981, incorporating a sub-matrix of the classification of combined growth rates for three decades.

The following points were taken into consideration while sampling:

(a) two major groups were taken, that is, growing villages (groups 1,3,6 of combined growth rates) and declining villages (groups 2,4,7); groups of 5,8 and 9 were omitted from the bivariate table;
(b) the villages having a minimum of population of 500 both in 1951 and 1981 were considered in the bivariate table;
(c) the villages having jumped size group from 1951 to 1981 were specially considered, e.g. Bechraji;
(d) spatial distribution was considered in selection of villages covering all six talukas;
(c) villages along highways and near railway stations as well as away from the same were selected;
(f) villages situated close to each other, one having increasing growth rate and the other having decreasing growth rate have been considered for sampling.

Out of a total of 546 villages, 53 villages (about 10 per cent) have been taken up for sampling. Dhinoj, in Chanasma taluka, despite having an average growth rate, is being studied as a special case as it has turned from urban to rural in 1981, according to the Census Report. A list of selected 53 villages is given in Appendix I.

3

PATTERN OF SETTLEMENTS

HUMAN beings locate themselves in a pattern on space. The development of such a pattern is the outcome of human decision and adjustment in response to physical and socio-economic factors. An analysis of the pattern or the structure is useful in understanding the processes that have brought about it and vice versa. Classification of a pattern into sub-sets leads to various measurements, and culminates in explanations of such a pattern. In this study, the locational pattern of settlements has been measured in various ways—at a point of time and over a period of time.

LORENZ CURVES

Lorenz curves have been used in the study (Figs. 3.1 and 3.2) to measure the pattern of concentration of settlements from Mahesana, the district headquarters, and from the second largest town, that is, Kalol, which is having a closer interaction with the external centres like Ahmedabad and Gandhinagar. The concentration of settlements is the highest between 35 and 45 per cent of distance from both the centres with respect to the line of 45°, suggesting the path of even distribution. Upto 10 per cent distance from Mahesana and Kalol, curves are close to each other, but after that, the concentration is higher in the case of Mahesana, value of R being .62, while it is low for Kalol (R=.46), suggesting more uniform distribution of settlements around Kalol.

In both the graphs, concentration of population is higher than that of the number of settlements (Fig. 3.2). The pattern

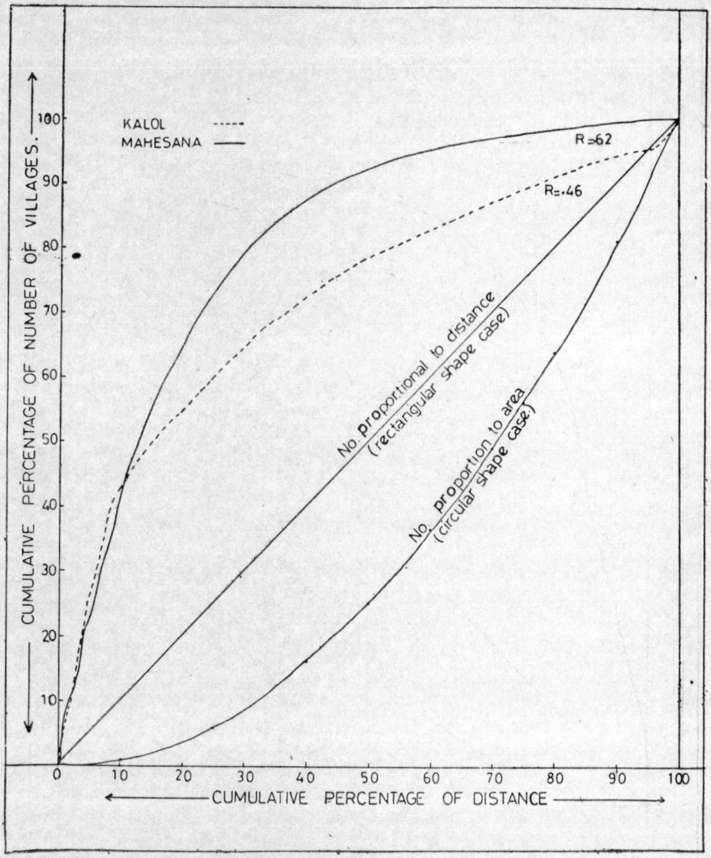

FIG. 3.1: *Lorenz curve showing the relation between distance and number of villages*

of curves remains unchanged, that is, the concentration is higher with respect to Mahesana (R=.72) than that of Kalol (R=.57). One of the reasons of higher concentration around Mahesana is that its location is more central than that of Kalol which is in the southern side of the study area. Moreover, the area concerned is not circular to have the total impact of the measurement of the Lorenz curve, where variables are cumulated in a concentric manner around a definite point. The two theoretical lines are based on the assumption of uniform distribution in a circular and a

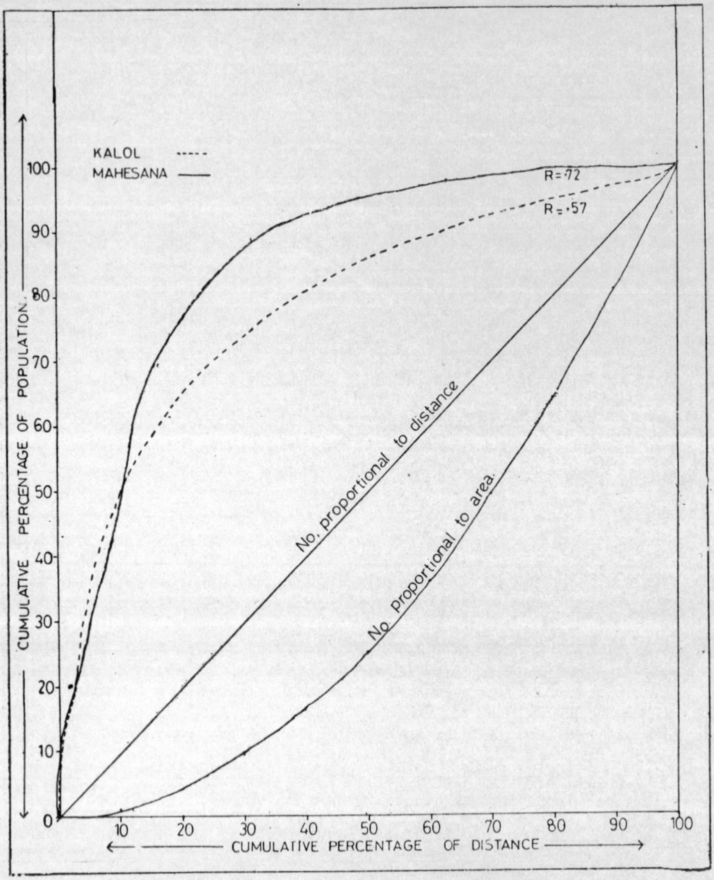

FIG. 3.2: *Lorenz curve showing the relation between distance and population*

rectangular area respectively. The rectangular model is more applicable for comparison of concentration in this study area.

NEAREST NEIGHBOUR ANALYSIS

Nearest neighbour analysis has been used to know the randomness in the distributional pattern of settlements. The ratio (R) of the observed mean distance and the expected mean distance between settlements varies from $R=0$, indicating clustering, $R=1$, suggesting random pattern and

TABLE 3.1 : **Nearest neighbour analysis**

Taluka	*No. of villages*	*Area km²*	*R—Value*	*Type of pattern*
Sami	97	1509.8	1.336	Random
Harij	40	407.0	1.455	Uniform
Chanasma	112	886.7	1.274	Random
Mahesana	110	791.4	1.236	Random
Kadi	118	829.7	1.383	Towards uniformity
Kalol	69	487.2	1.540	Uniform
Total (Towns included)	546	4911.80	1.279	Random

R=2.15, indicating uniformity (Table 3.1 and Map 3.1). In general, any pattern takes a value which is often not exactly 0, 1 or 2.15; so an approximate range has been used to categorize the talukas which are the units of area in this nearest neighbour analysis (details are in Chapter 2). Kalol has the highest R value, suggesting a distribution towards uniformity, Kadi and Harij also have shown the same tendency. The uniform distribution indicates that the factors controlling the pattern have a uniform impact on them, whereas randomness in Mahesana, Chanasma and Sami talukas implies that there are no strong factors affecting such a pattern. The approximate range, taken here, is:

$R = <.71$ (clustering), $R = .71$ to 1.42 (random),
$R = > 1.42$ (uniformity)

MEAN CENTRE VS POPULATION CENTRE

The centre of gravity is different from that of the administrative one. The mean area centre is at Palej, whereas the mean population centre is at Santhal. Both the villages are in Mahesana taluka. Mahesana, perhaps, could have been the mean centre and mean population centre, had the study area been the whole district. The study area includes only six southern talukas out of 11 talukas of the district. Though Mahesana is the administrative centre, Kalol, having large

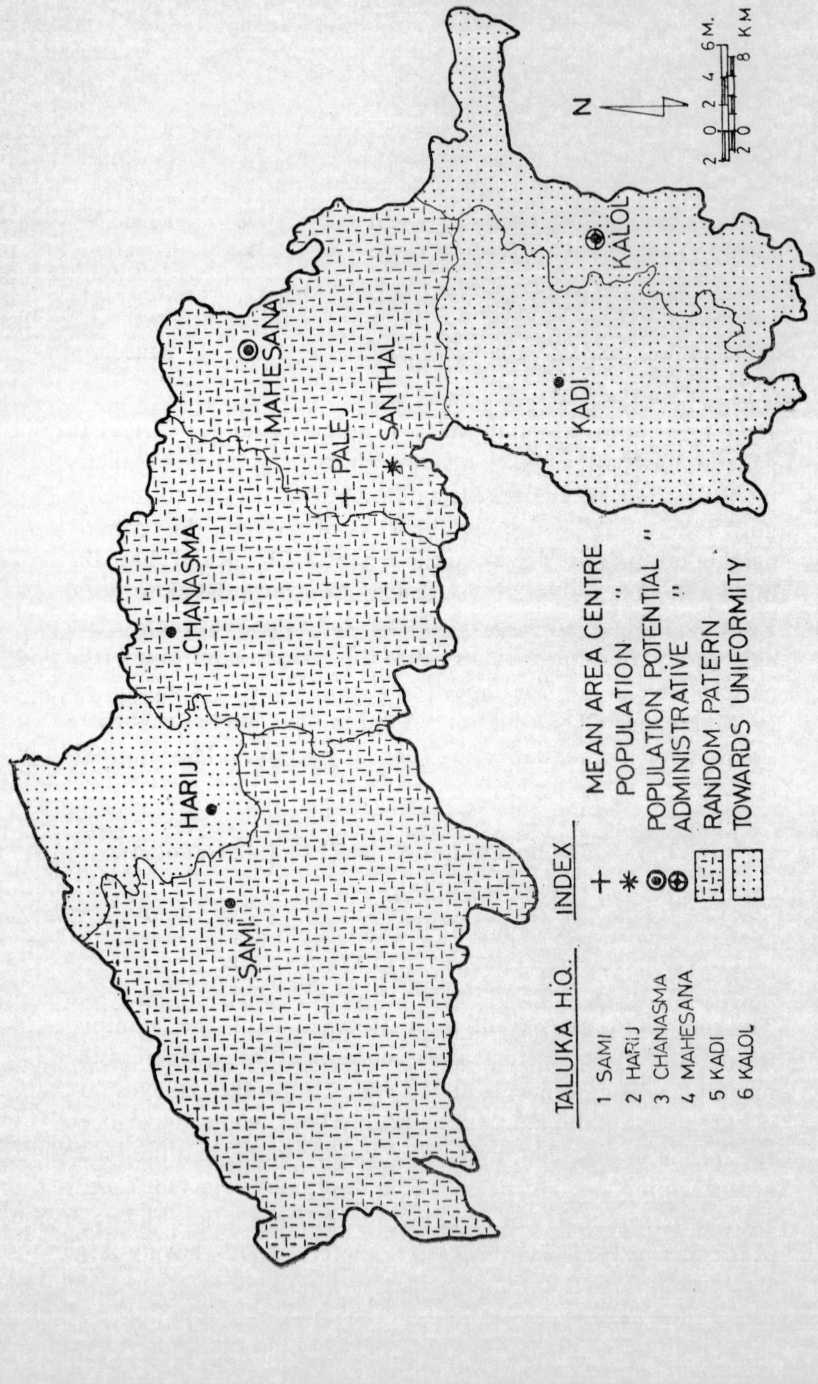

MAP 3.1: *Nearest neighbour distribution and centre of gravity (1981)*

and closely spaced villages around it, is the population potential centre.

POPULATION POTENTIAL

Using the idea of gravitation, potential of a village, or a node, is a measure of proximity of that village to all other villages in the region. In other words, potential of a centre is an aggregate measure of influence of all other centres as proportional to the mass of all centres and inversely proportional to the distance from them. A village is expected to have a high potential value if it is surrounded with large villages which will be responsible for socio-economic interactions (Ref. 1, 8, 21). The sum of all influence of mass and distance can be depicted as a continuous spatial variable in the form of contours (potential surface). In this study, total population of villages has been considered as the mass, and the distance is measured in kilometres in linear form (details are given in Chapter 2). Mass can be any other variable, e.g. retail sales, income, etc., and distance can be measured in terms of time or cost or by non-linear road distance.

Theoretically it is expected that, in a distribution, interaction will be proportionally high if the mass is large in centres and it will be inversely low with increasing distance between centres. If any one of these two variables changes, interaction changes in the system. These elements, in a set of population centres, exert their influence on all other centres. In the study area, keeping the distance as constant, the impact of population or mass on potential of each village has been analysed over a period of three decades (Maps 3.2 and 3.3) with the help of computer programming. As the mass changes by decade so does the population potential value of the village. In 1951, a large portion of the study area has a population potential of less than 27,000, it varied between 27,000 and 47,000 in Mahesana and Kalol talukas. The value was very high, forming a loop near the town of Kalol. The minimum potential was 8,349 at Adagam village in Sami and the maximum 1,29,626 at Kalol (Map 3.2). In 1961, the population potential value increased in the west in Chanasma taluka, ranging between 27,000 and 47,000, and the high

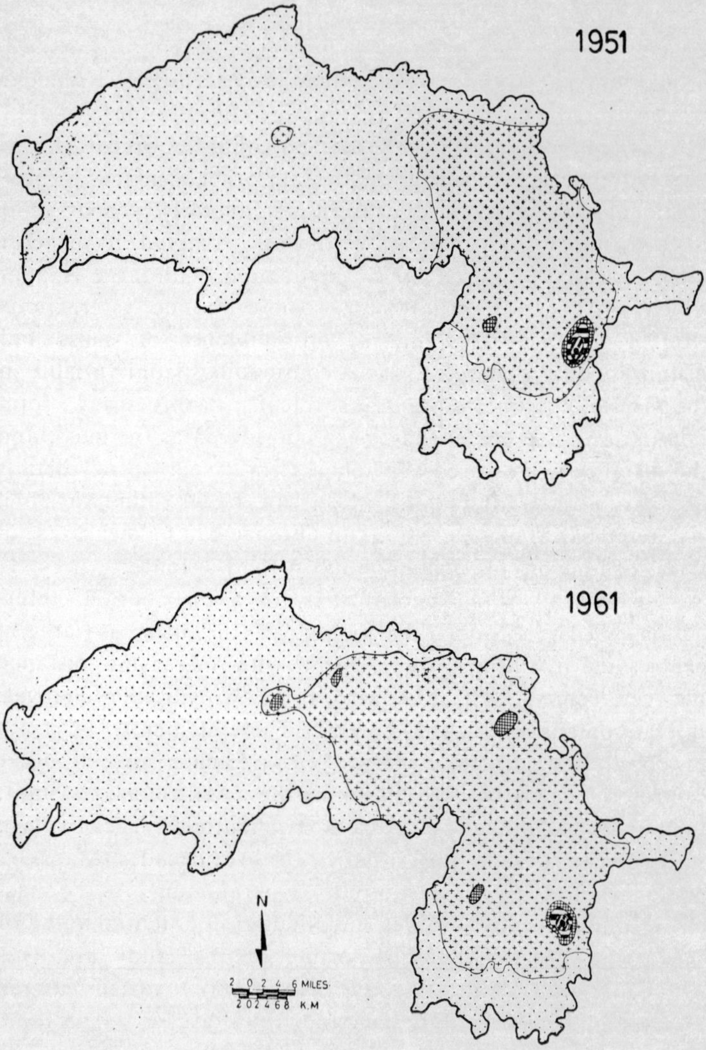

MAP 3.2: *Population potential surface (1951-1961)*

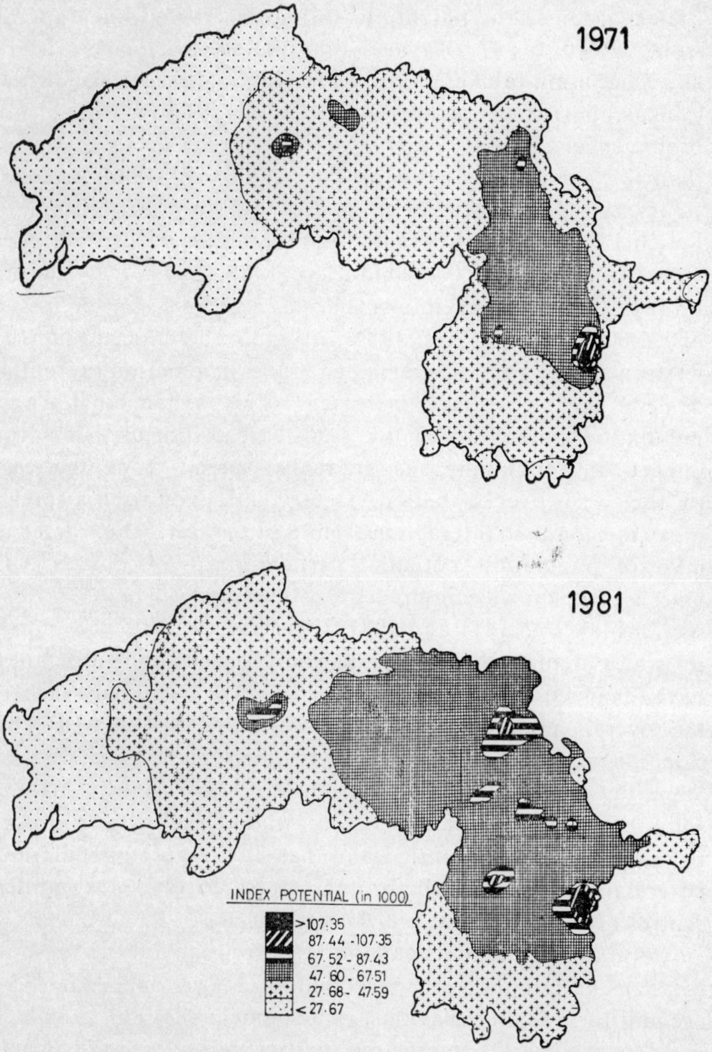

MAP 3.3: *Population potential surface (1971-81)*

loop was still existing near Kalol. Few loops of high potential values varying between 47,000 and 67,000 were visible around Kadi, Mahesana, Dhinoj and Chanasma. In 1971, the extension of the potential was mainly in the value ranging from 27,000 to 47,000, and the spread took place in Harij and Chanasma talukas (Map 3.3). In Mahesana and Kalol talukas, potential surface of 47,000 to 67,000 came into prominence. Finally, in 1981, the potential value lower than 27,000 was not visible in Kadi and Kalol talukas. It is seen only in western Sami, near the Little Rann of Kutch. The loops of potential got strengthened with higher values of 67,000 to 1,04,000 in Kalol, Mahesana and Chanasma talukas. Even Sami taluka had a higher potential value of 27,000 to 47,000 in 1981. It is to be noticed that the western side of Sami has remained low in population potential while other areas have increased. This dynamic pattern of population potential, in the study area, indicates how the impact of population has gradually spread from the east to the west over a period of 30 years, indicating a spread of socio-economic interaction from east to west. The isometric map of population potential surfaces of 1981 (Map 3.4) gives a three-dimension impact of it in terms of height. Cross-sections taken in 1951 and 1981 from west to east and north to south depict the height of the surface, and show how they have changed over time (Fig. 3.3). As explained earlier, the overall potential had increased much in 30 years. The slope in cross-sections increases gradually from the west, in Sami, to the east in Kalol. Potential cross-sections show a small height in Mahesana if it is drawn from north to south. In all the cross-sections, Kalol has the highest population potential indicating a high interaction pattern with other centres of large size that are closely spaced.

Population potentials cannot, however, explain the reasons of their variation over space and are also inadequate to account for human behaviour. The model is helpful in understanding the overall interaction impact of size and distance of a centre with respect to all other centres in a region, thereby analysing settlements in a systems approach.

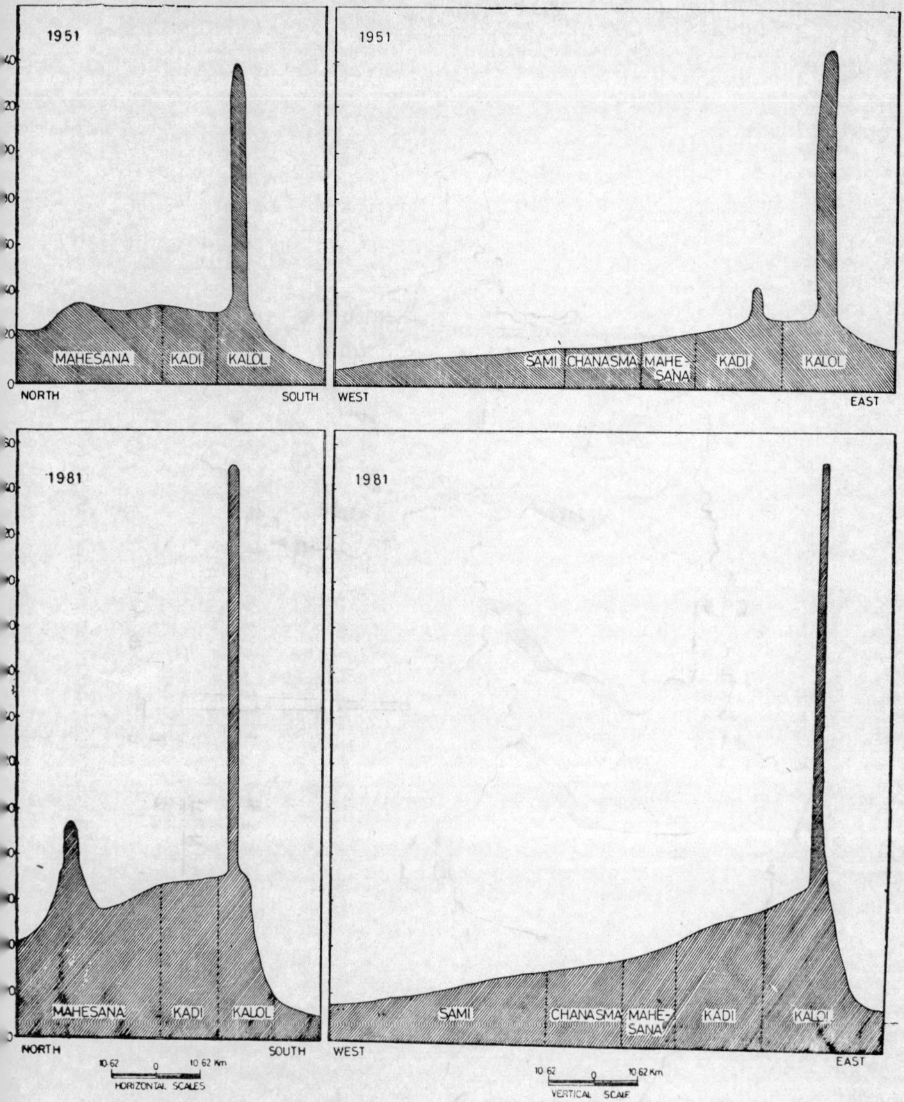

FIG. 3.3: *Gradient of population potential*

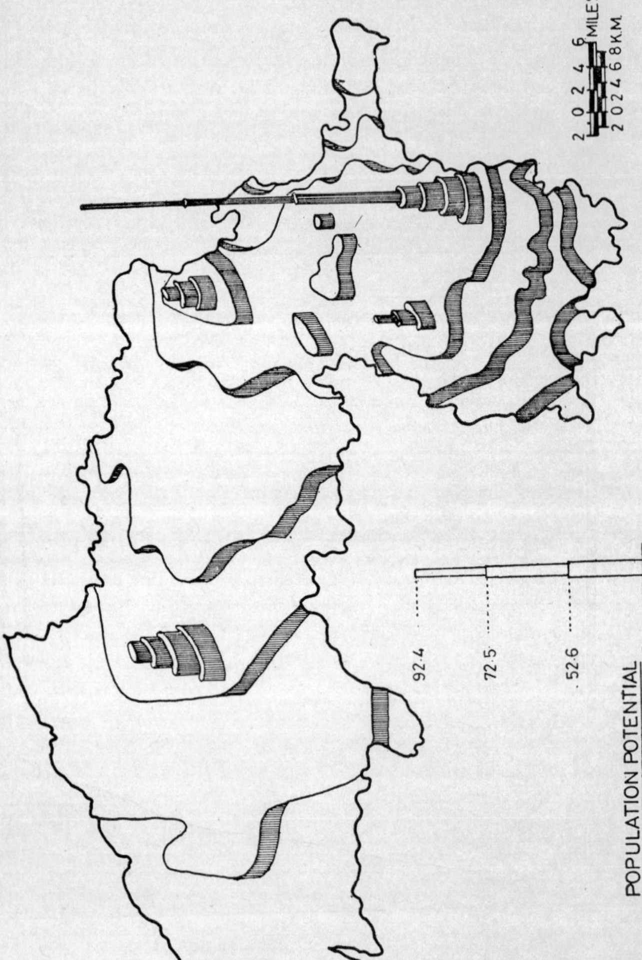

MAP 3.4: *Isometric population potential (1981)*

RANK-SIZE DISTRIBUTION

Rank-size relationship help us understand the hierarchy of size of population that exists within the settlement system of an area. The rank-size rule establishes a relationship such as the population of the nth settlement is $1/n^{th}$ the size of the largest settlement's (p_1) population, thereby the expected line of rank-size rule has a slope of —1 on a log scale, that is

$$P_n = \frac{P_1}{n}.$$

The distortions in the hierarchical pattern of settlements can be pointed out by comparing the actual rank-size distribution with that of the expected one (Fig. 3.4). Moreover, the stability or changes in the settlement system, in terms of rank and size, are other useful aspects of study. The minimum population considered here in rank-size is 3,000 in 1951 and 4,000 in 1981. In the study area, in 1951, among the 45 most populated settlements, a trinary system appears, showing a plateau with three towns of first group, Mahesana, Kalol and Kadi, then there is a fall of second group of settlements and gradually the distribution of third group of villages remains above the expected line. The system indicates that three towns on the eastern side have competitive position. Relatively small villages of the third group are more in number than those of second size group. In 1981, the rank-size line remains almost parallel to that of 1951 with few changes, firstly, Kalol became more important in size than Kadi, so the plateau has become binary with Mahesana and Kalol being important centres. A sharp change of slope occurs after the two centres, though the relative position of Kadi has remained the same. Secondly, the mid-size group has gone below the expected line and those of smaller size have come closer to the expected line, though their position is above it. In other words, the observed rank-size rule has shifted closer to that of the expected one over 30 years among the top 45 settlements in the study area.

Rank-size distribution has been prepared for two talukas separately with 30 most populated settlements, having different physical and economic background over three decades

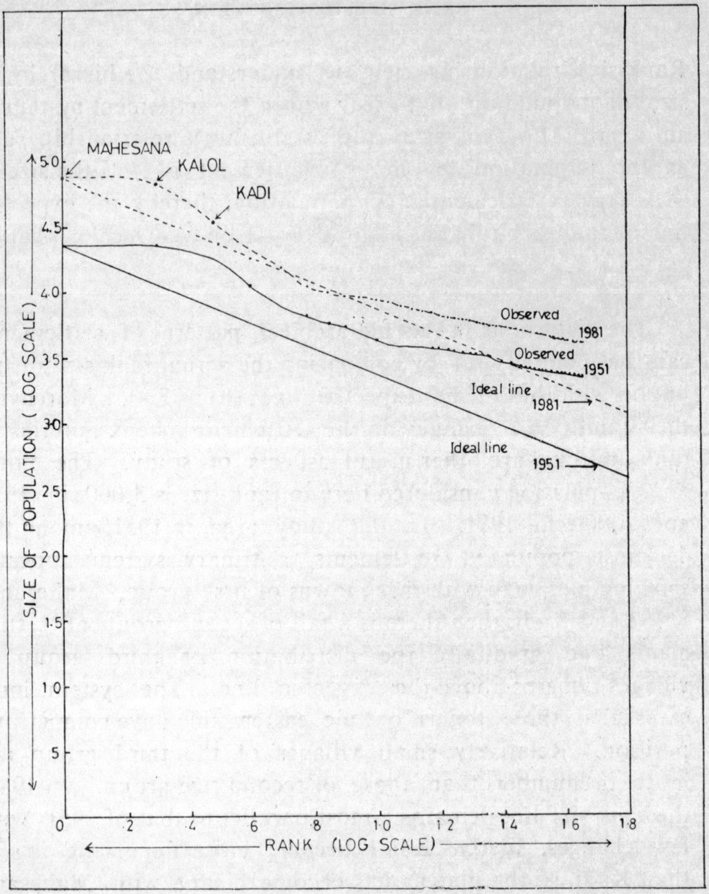

FIG. 3.4: *Rank-size distribution of the study area*

(Figs. 3.5 and 3.6). Sami has a low rainfall, low irrigation and is relatively poor economically. The situation is reverse for Kalol taluka. Both the systems, in talukas with and without irrigation, that is, Kalol and Sami respectively, have shown regularity, though the pattern itself is different. In Kalol, primate system is visible and the strong importance of Kalol increased in 1981 with a high population potential. The relatively smaller settlements, which were above the expected rank-size line in 1951, went below the line in 1981, suggesting a growth of relatively small villages lower than what is expected.

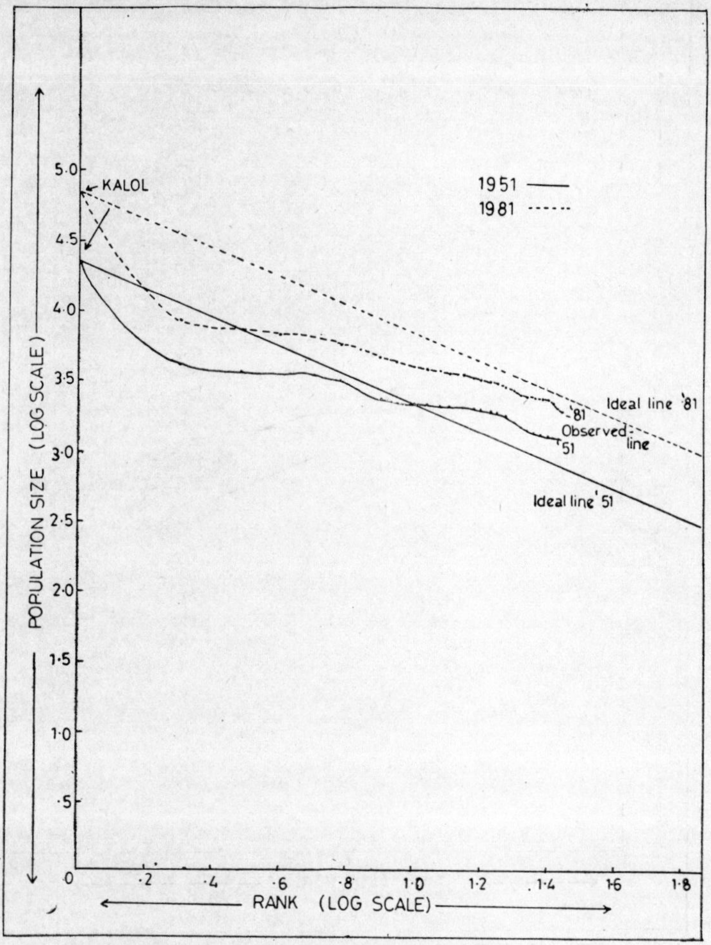

FIG. 3.5: *Rank-size distribution in Kalol taluka*

In Sami taluka, the rank-size distribution is quite different from that of Kalol taluka. Firstly, since there is no town in Sami taluka, there is no primacy; the observed distribution for the first few ranks is very close to the expected one; relatively medium and smaller centres have gone above the expected line of distribution suggesting higher growth than what is expected. In general, the system has shown a stable distribution during 1951-1981, having the rank-size line parallel to each other. In general, a high degree of primacy

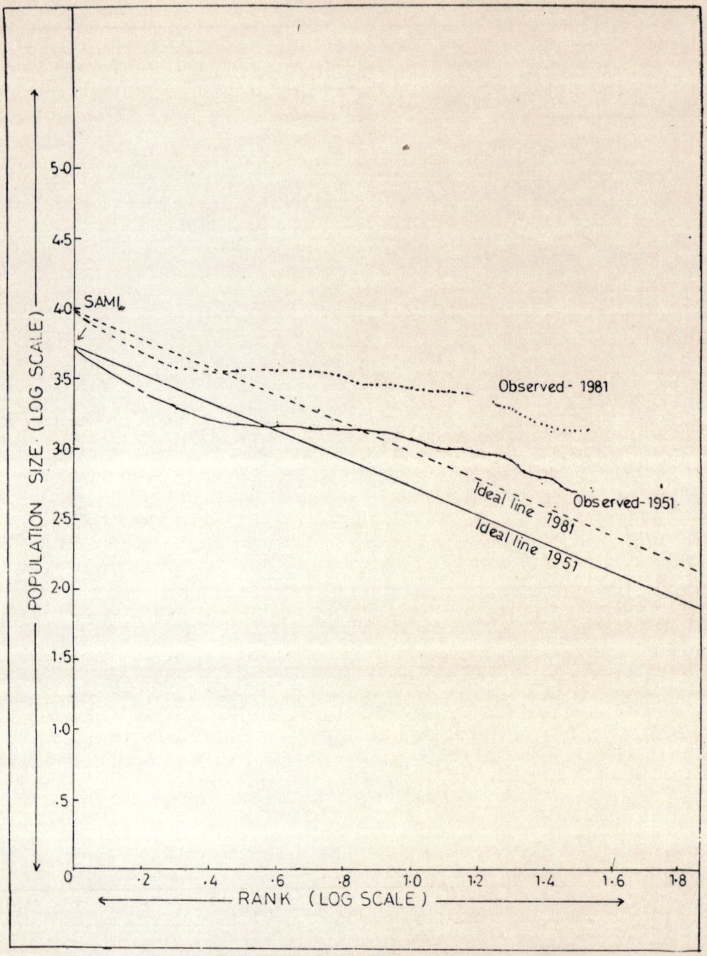

FIG. 3.6: *Rank-size distribution in Sami taluka*

is considered to be indicative of a strong centre with other settlements of low level of spatial interaction. In the study area, there is an indication of primacy of Kalol with high interaction and high population potential, high density with high connectivity and good relative location. In Sami, there is a predominance of very small centres without any town in the taluka. In Sami, smaller settlements have populations above the expected size. In short, the Kalol area has indicated a touch of primacy while such a prominant centre is lacking in the taluka of Sami.

4

DEMOGRAPHIC ASPECTS

THE pattern of settlements is very much associated with its demographic aspects—its distribution, size, density, growth-rate and composition. An analysis of various aspects of demography in settlements helps us understand the processes that have been responsible for it. This chapter deals with demographic aspects while the processes are explained in the following chapter.

DISTRIBUTION

The distribution and evolution of the distribution of settlements bring out clearly the interaction between people on space in a particular environment.

Both the distribution of villages and of population are not even in the study area. The number of villages and their population gradually increase from west in Sami taluka to east in Mahesana and Kalol talukas (Table 4.1 and 4.2 (Sami). taluka covers 30 per cent of the total study area but it has only 18 per cent of villages. The expected number of villages is 166 in relation to its area. In the eastern side, Mahesana, Kadi and Kalol, the observed number of villages are more than expected (Table 4.1). The situation is same in terms of population (1981). Both Sami and Harij have a low percentage of population compared to the expected population in terms of their area (Table 4.1). Chanasma's observed population is equal to its expected figure, while Mahesana, Kadi and Kalol have more population than the expected figures. The hypothesis is accepted by Chi-Square test at a confidence

TABLE 4.1 : **Chi-square test on the distribution of villages by taluka (1981)**

Taluka	Area (km^2)	Per cent of area (observed)	Observed No. of villages	Per cent of villages (observed)	Expected No. of villages	Per cent of expected No. of villages
Sami	1509.8	30.74	97	17.96	166	30.74
Harij	407.0	8.29	39	7.23	45	8.33
Chanasma	886.0	18.04	110	20.37	97	17.96
Mahesana	791.4	16.11	109	20.18	87	16.11
Kadi	829.7	16.89	117	21.66	91	16.86
Kalol	487.2	9.93	68	12.60	54	10.00
Total	4911.10	100.00	540	100.00	540	100.00

N.B. : Towns are excluded.

TABLE 4.2 : **Chi-square test on the distribution of population by taluka (1981)**

Taluka	Area (km^2)	Per cent of area	Observed population (1981)	Per cent of population	Expected population (1981)	Per cent of expected population
Sami	1509.8	30.74	128000	11.18	351749	30.74
Harij	407.0	8.29	69000	6.03	94809	8.29
Chanasma	886.0	18.04	207000	18.09	206390	18.04
Mahesana	791.4	16.11	305000	26.66	184260	16.11
Kadi	829.7	16.89	215000	18.79	193346	16.89
Kalol	487.2	9.93	220000	19.25	113446	9.93
Total	4911.10	100.00	1144000	100.00	1144000	100.00

level of 95 per cent that there is a difference in the distribution of villages and population by the area of talukas.

The uneven distribution of population is visible on the

maps of population distribution of 1951 and 1981 (Maps 4.1 and 4.2). Three towns of Mahesana, Kadi and Kalol had populations ranging from 15,000 to 25,000 in 1951, while Sami, Harij and Chanasma had it from 5,000 to 15,000. In 1981, the hierarchy of population developed with Mahesana and Kalol as important, large town in the east, Kadi comes next in size; then a number of settlements have grown along the line of communication near the highway and railway line, having a size between 5,000 and 15,000.

SIZE OF SETTLEMENTS

The size of settlements often is an indicator of the economic prosperity of an area (Ref. Nos. 1,2). Theoretically, by Rank-size Rule, one can expect to have a distribution of large number of settlements of small size and a fewer number of cities of large size. But in the study area, settlements with a smaller size increase in number with increasing size, then the number decreases with increasing size (Fig. 4.1). Secondly, the mode of distribution is shifting to the right from 200 to 299 in 1951 to 500 to 999 in 1961. The mode remained same in 1971, then it shifted to the size group of 1000 to 1999. Thirdly, there has been an overall decline in the number of villages with size varying between 500 and 999. The decline in the number of villages has taken place also in the group of 200-499. The size group of 500-999 is a transitional zone where there has been both an increase and a decrease of number. There has been an increase in the number in the group of 1000-1999 to that of more than 10,000, the highest increase is seen in the size group of 2000-4999.

The change in size-group of settlement can be visualized better in a bivariate table (Table 4.3). As stated earlier, the differential in the increase in number, during 1951-1981, is in the group of 2000-4999. The majority of these settlements was having a population between 1,000 and 1,999 in 1951. Ninety settlements out of 119 have increased in size from 1000-1999 group to 2000-4999 group, but 27 of them remained in the same group, that is, in the original group (Table 4.3). These 90 villages which have grown faster in size are found in all talukas, including quite a few in southern

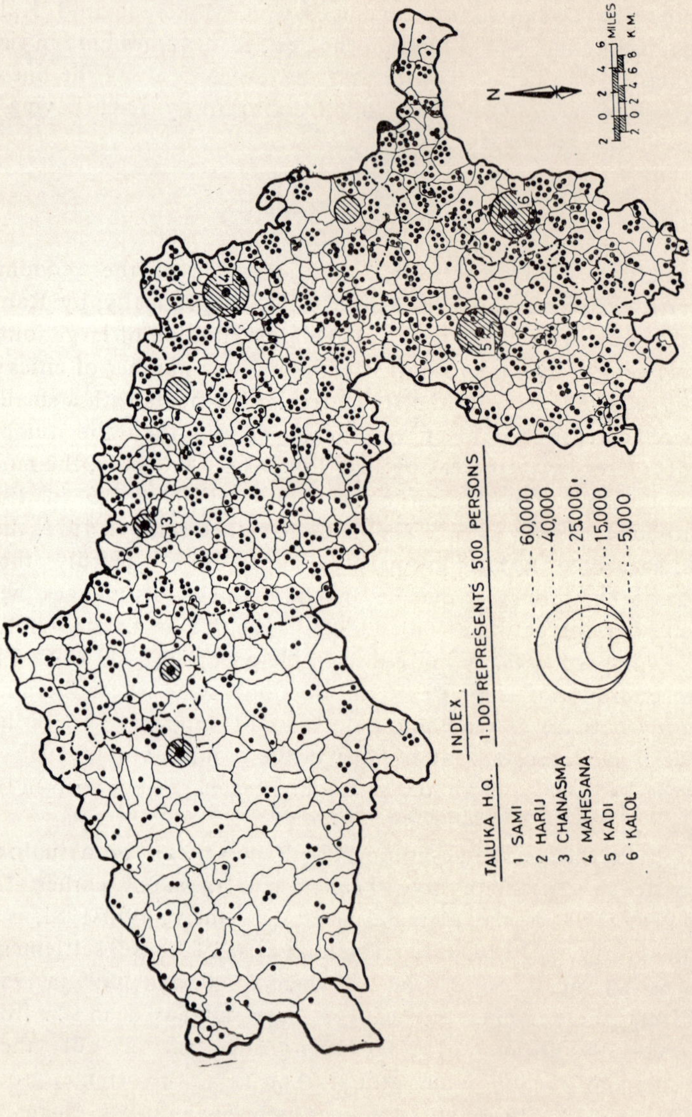

MAP 4.1: *Distribution of population (1951)*

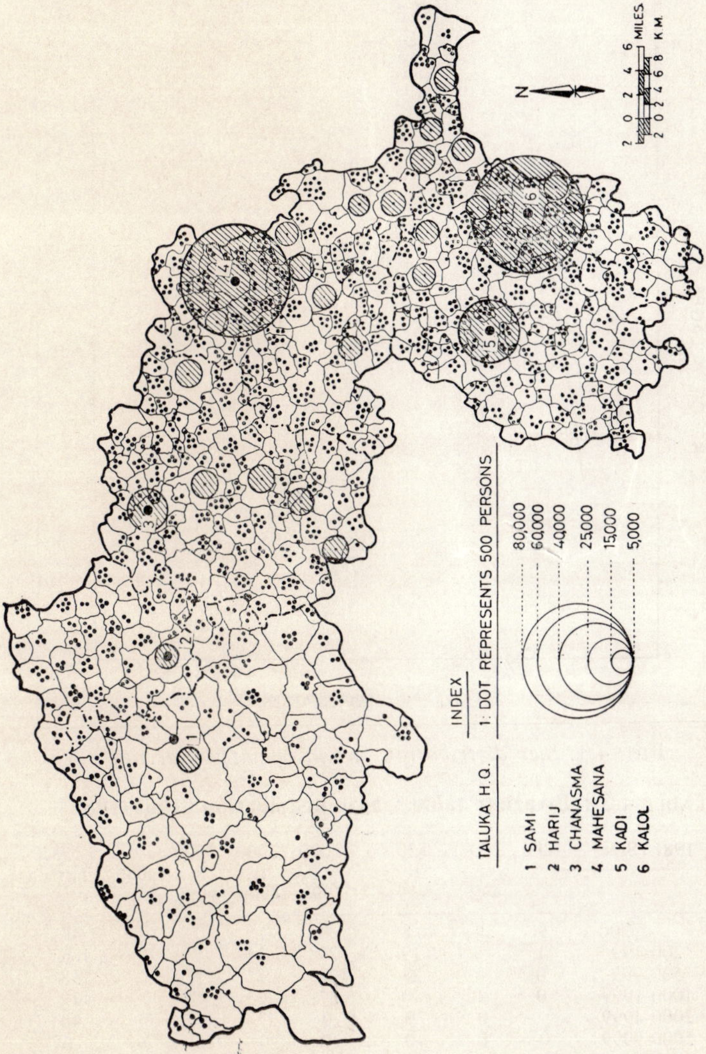

MAP 4.2: *Distribution of population (1981)*

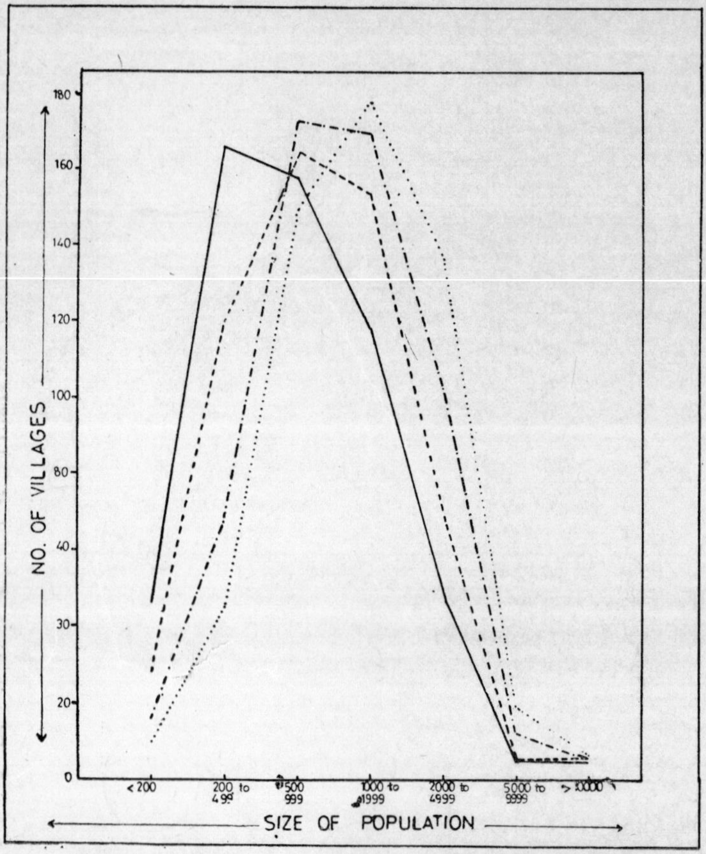

FIG. 4.1: *Size distribution of settlements by decade*

TABLE 4.3 : Bivariate table : Size distribution (1951-1981)

1981 (Size) →	<200	200 to 499	500 to 999	1000 to 1999	2000 to 4999	5000 to 9999	10000 +	1951 Total
1951 Size ↓ <200	9	29	8*	0	1*	0	0	47
200-499	1	16	119	29*	1*	0	0	166
500-999	0	0	23	122	12*	1*	0	158
1000-1999	0	1	0	27	90	1*	0	119
2000-4999		0	0	0	33	15	0	48
5000-9999	0	0	0	0	0	2	2	4
10000+	0	0	0	0	0	0	4	4
1981 Total	10	46	150	178	137	19	6	546

*Settlements that jumped one size-class.

Source : *District Census Handbook*, 1951, 1981

Sami. Some of them have availability of water, while some are on the highway from Patan to Viramgam. They are quite random in distribution, but many of them are well connected, having good irrigation facility or good amenities.

The distribution of size-group varies over time and space (Fig. 4.2). In Kalol taluka with more rainfall and irrigation, a plateau type of distribution is noticed with bimodal type in 1951, having both small and medium settlements with a very large primate town of Kalol. The primary mode has shifted from 200-499 group in 1951 to 2000-4999 in 1981. In 1981, there was no distinct secondary mode as in 1951. Sami taluka, with a dry climate and little irrigation, has a different type of size distribution. It has a single mode which has shifted from 200-499 to 500-999. There has been a decline of number up to the size of 200-499 during 1951-1981, then the number increases from 500-999 group with increasing size (Fig. 4.2) in 1981. The dry area has a larger number of small-size settlements. The distribution of settlements in Fig. 4.2 includes all settlements in Kalol and Sami talukas, whereas Rank-size distribution in Figs. 3.5 and 3.6 has been prepared for only 33 settlements from the top by size.

The growth of urban population is related to that of size (Table 4.4). There is no urban centre in Sami. Chanasma

TABLE 4.4 : **Per cent of urban population to total population by taluka**

Taluka	1951	1961	1971	1981 (estimated)
Sami	Nil	Nil	Nil	Nil
Harij	20.69	20.36	20.07	21.60
Chanasma	15.34	14.00	8.26	7.40
Mahesana	15.35	17.32	20.96	18.43
Kadi	16.54	16.11	15.27	16·02
Kalol	21.07	24.44	29.17	36.39

Source : *District Census Handbook*, 1951, 1961, 1971.

has indicated a decline of urban population, as Dhinoj has been termed rural from urban in 1981. Harij and Kadi have a steady growth, Mahesana shows a moderate growth while Kalol has a fast rate of growth in urban population due to

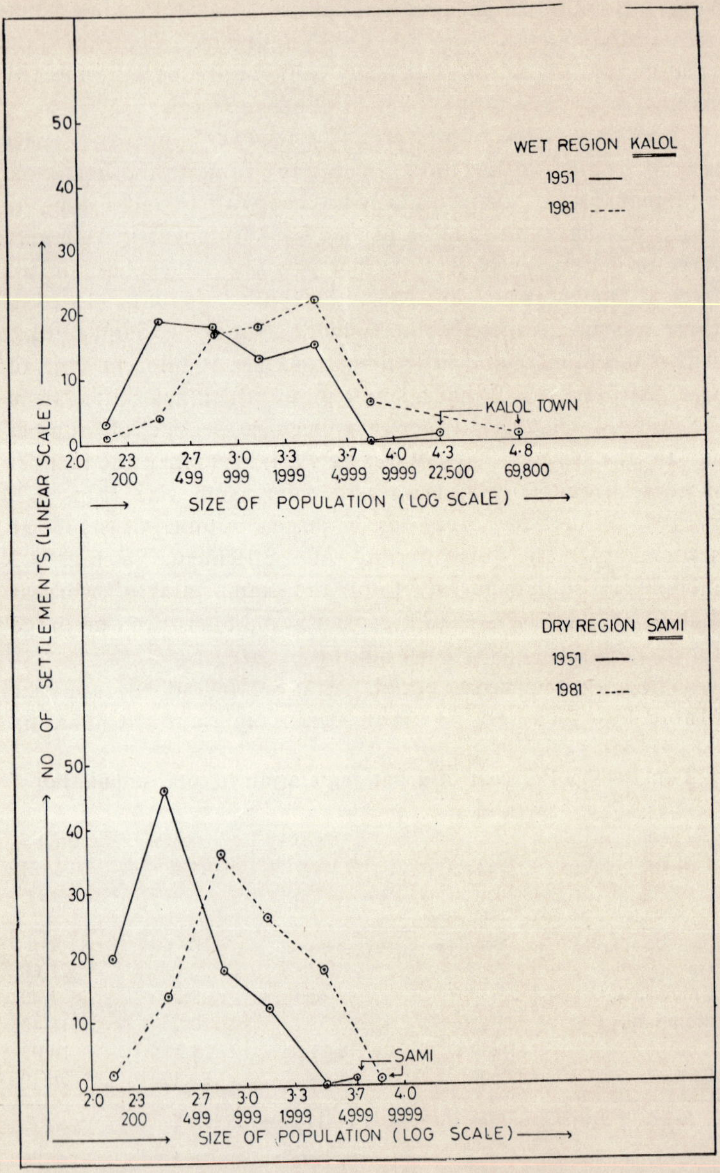

FIG. 4.2: *Distribution of settlements in wet and dry regions*

irrigation, non-primary activities, good connectivity which are explained in the next chapter.

DENSITY

Density of persons per unit of area represents the ratio of man to land. In 1951, the whole of Sami and Harij talukas had low density (Map 4.3). The low density zone extends in the southern part of Chanasma and south-western parts of Kadi and Kalol talukas. Moderate to high density areas are in the north-eastern parts of Mahesana and Kalol talukas. The relative situation was the same, even after 30 years, in 1981 (Map 4.4), though the average density has increased in 1951-1981. It is interesting to note that the per cent change in density of persons per square kilometre is moderate to high in Sami, Harij and south Chanasma talukas where density as such was low both in 1951 and in 1981. The per cent change is low in Mahesana and Kalol where the density was high, both in 1951 and in 1981 (Table 4.5 and Map 4.5).

TABLE 4.5 : **Bivariate table of density : 1951-1981**

1981→ / 1951↓	Low	Average	Moderate	High	Total
Low	220	24	3	Nil	247
Average	19	111	22	7	159
Moderate	3	20	42	16	31
High	4	3	9	37	53
Total	246	158	76	60	540

N.B. : Towns have been excluded.
Source : *District Census Handbook*, 1951, 1981 (estimated).

Density of population in 1981 has been regressed with population potential values (1981), and residuals have been mapped to show the departure between the two (Map 4.6). The area with + and — ½ standard deviation of the regression line has been considered as the "normal zone". The areas having more density than + ½ S.D. is taken as "above normal" and that below — ½ S.D. is "below normal" density. The residual map brings out the same picture with below normal density in the Sami-Harij area, and also the south and western parts of Chanasma, Mahesana and Kadi talukas, while the density, above normal, is visible in the north and eastern areas in Mahesana and Kalol talukas. The residual mapping is an

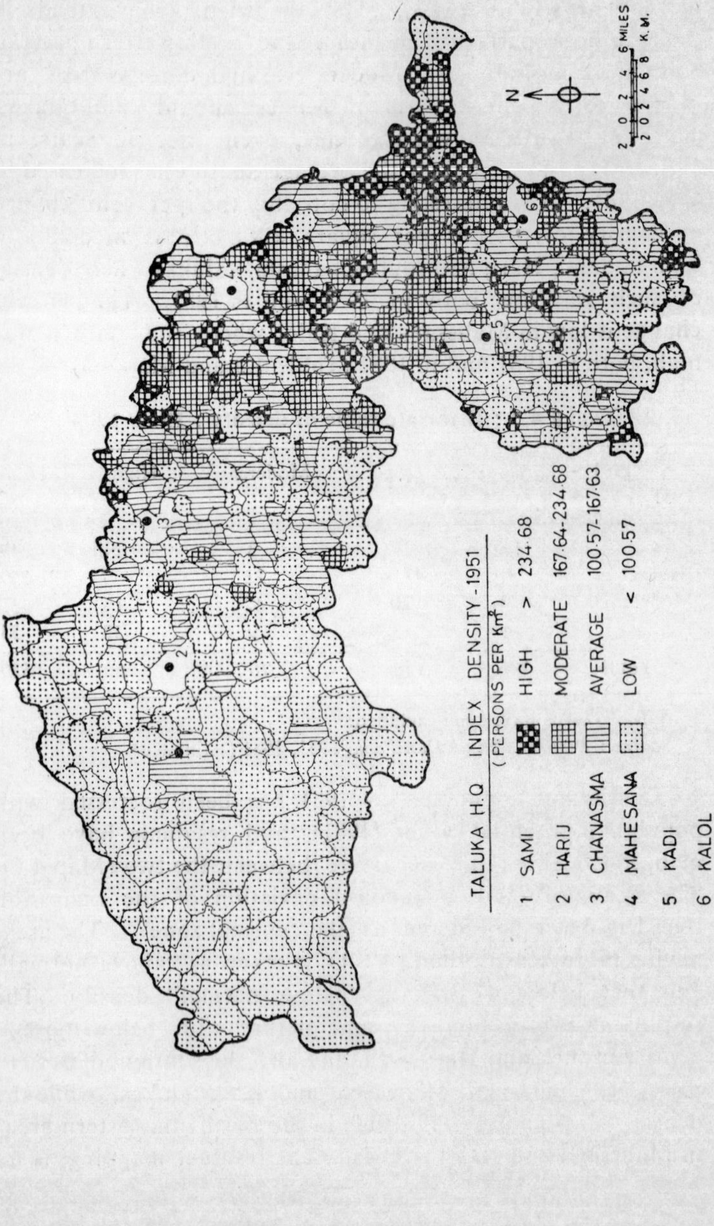

MAP 4.3 : *Density of population (1951)*

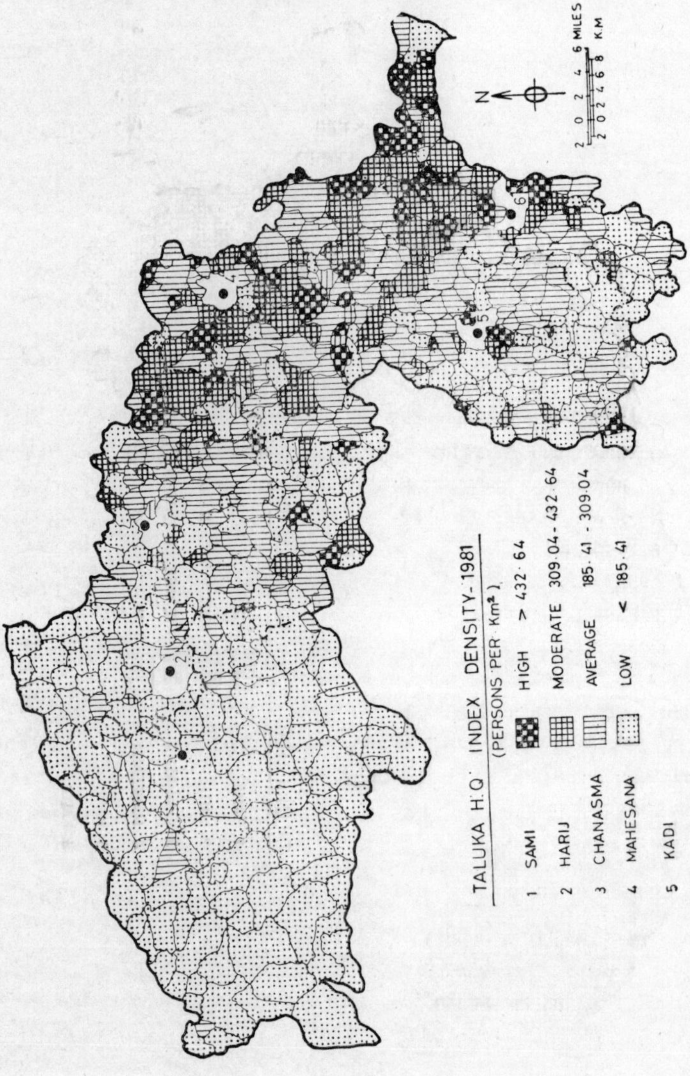

MAP 4.4: *Density of population (1981)*

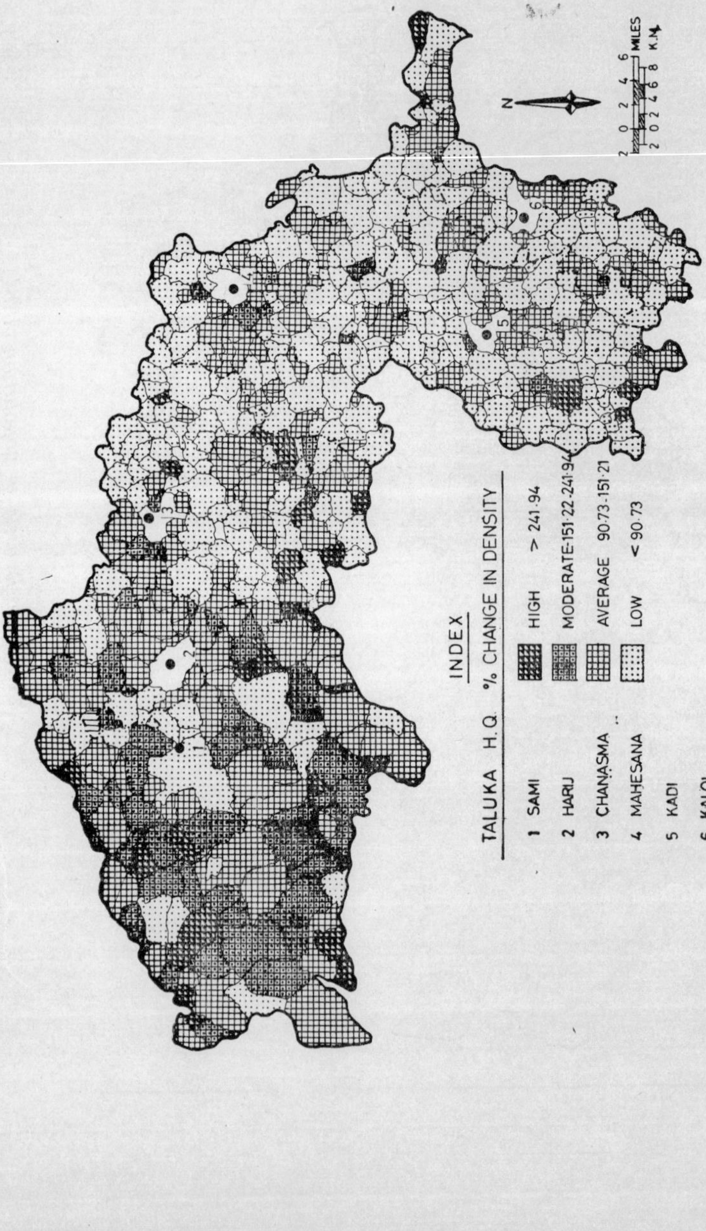

MAP 4.5: *Change in density: 1951-81*

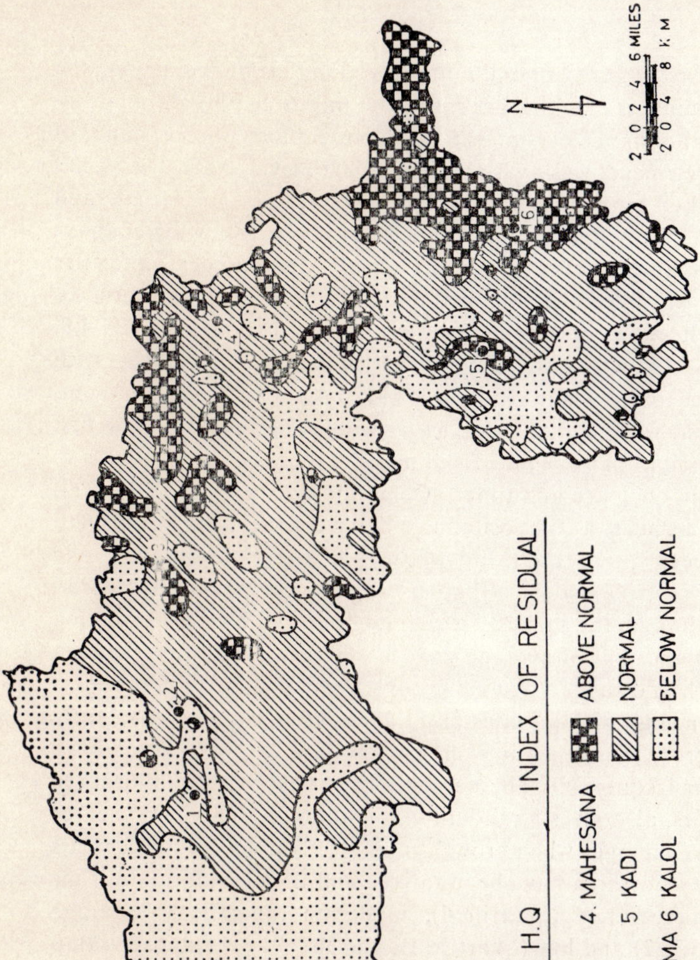

MAP 4.6: *Residual map of population potential and density (1981)*

indicator of areas for further investigation of factors for above and below normal areas.

GROWTH RATE

The growth rate of population is a complex phenomenon, the determinants of which are birth rate minus death rate and in-migration minus out-migration of population. Since none of these elements was available at village level, this study has described growth rate with maps and tables over time and space. The analysis is carried out in the following chapter. As explained earlier, in Chapter 2 of Methodology, quartiles of growth have been mapped to know the spatial variation of growth rates of population by decade (Maps 4.7, 4.8, 4.9, 4.10). Growth rates have been examined by taluka, with respect to the whole study area (Map 4.11) and also in comparison with the district as a whole (Map 4.12). The first impression that one gets from maps is that the growth rate is random on space and time. Combining the growth rate of all three decades, a composite map, depicting the nature of growth has been prepared (Map 4.10). A classification of nine groups, explained in Chapter 2, has been made. Mixed growth has the highest frequency, followed by the fluctuating group and that of average growth. Decreasingly low, sudden growth and sudden decline groups have a similar frequency. Settlements with a constantly high growth rate, constantly low growth rate and decreasingly low growth rate, have similar frequency. The nature of growth rate combining three decades, also gives a random distribution on space. A clearer picture emerges when growth rates (1971-81) of all settlements in the study area have been ranked and then divided into four quartiles, as high (quartile 4), moderate (quartile 3), average (quartile 2) and low (quartile 1), and then it is mapped (Map 4.11). The percentage of high growth rates (quartile 4) is largest in Sami, i.e. 40 per cent, followed by Chanasma (19 per cent), whereas the percentage of low growth rate (quartile 1) is low in Sami and high in Kadi (33 per cent) and Mahesana (23 per cent).

Finally, the growth rate of settlements has been compared with that of the district (1971-1981). A pattern emerges from

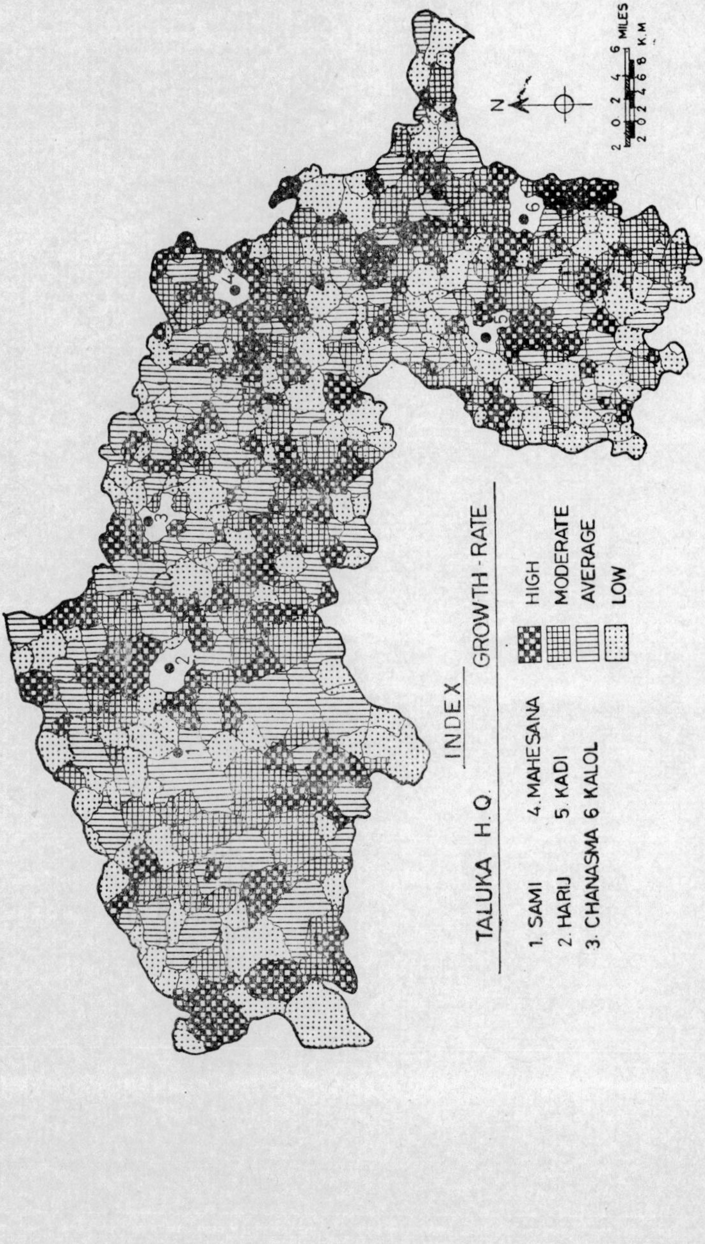

MAP 4.7: *Growth rate of population (1951-1961)*

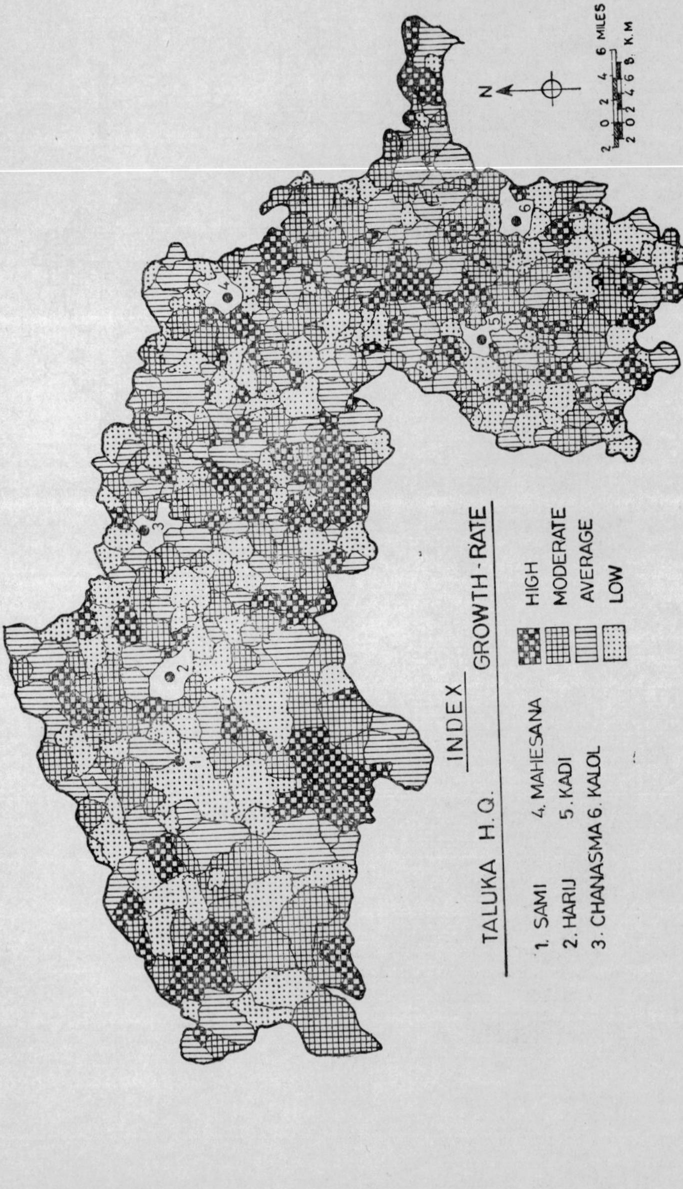

MAP 4.8: *Growth rate of population (1961-1971)*

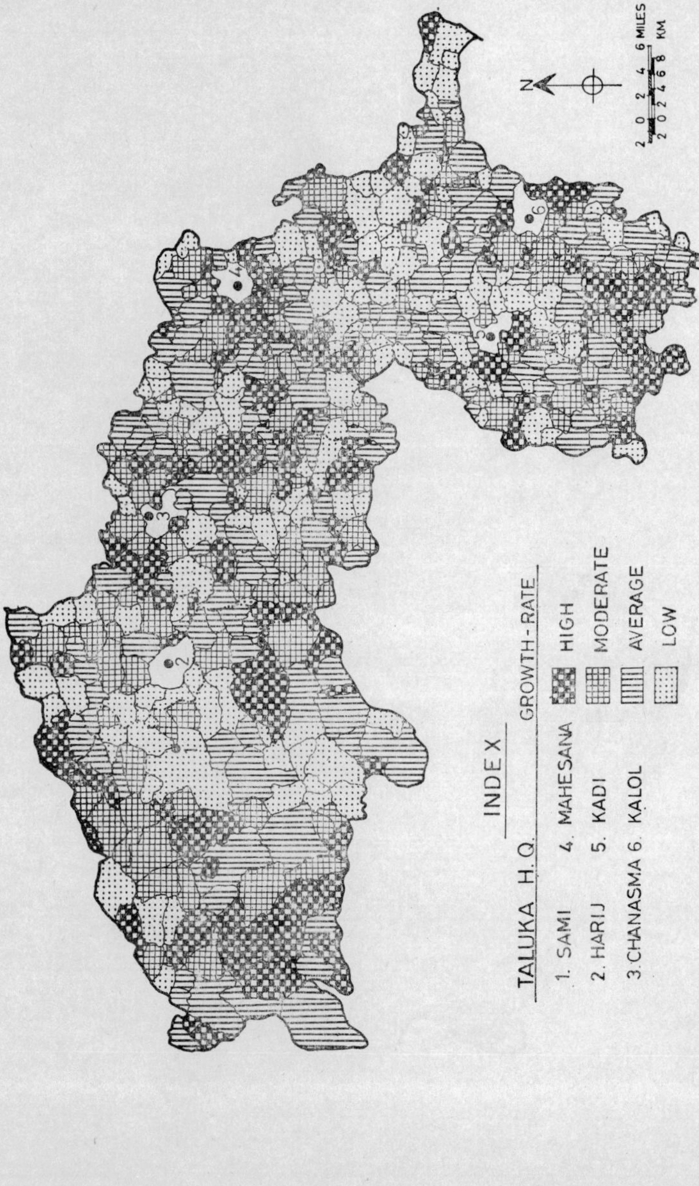

MAP 4.9: *Growth rate of population (1971-1981)*

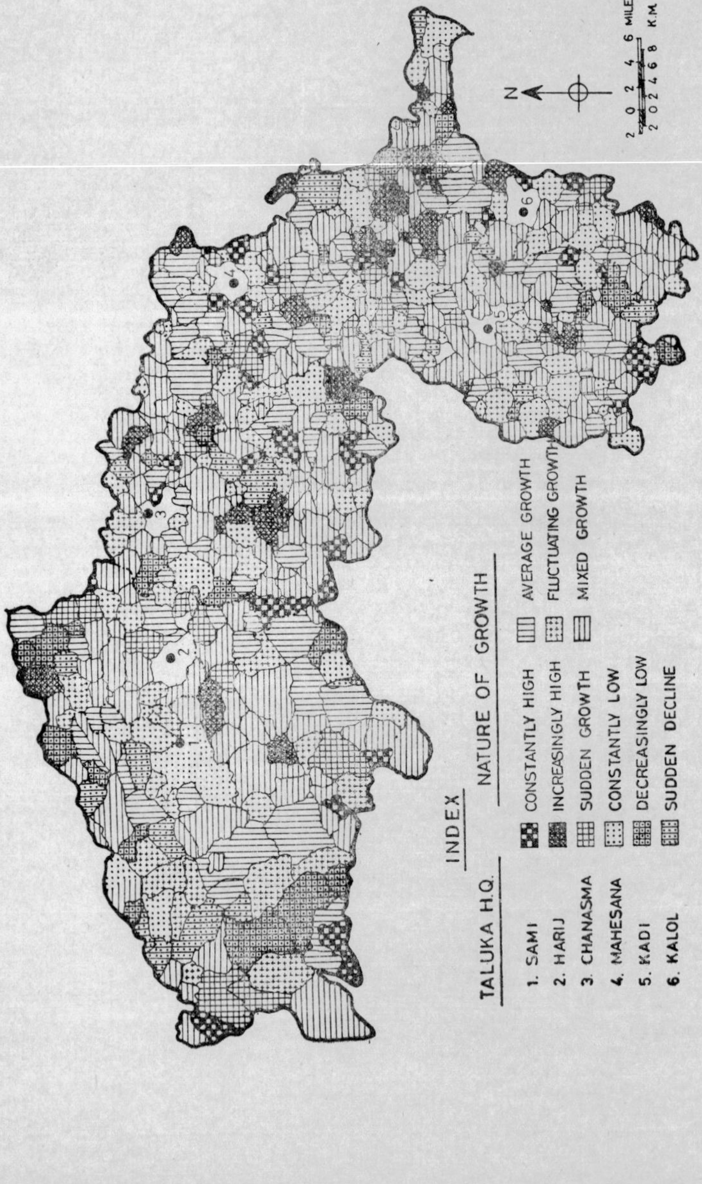

MAP 4.10: *Nature of growth rate of population (1951-1981)*

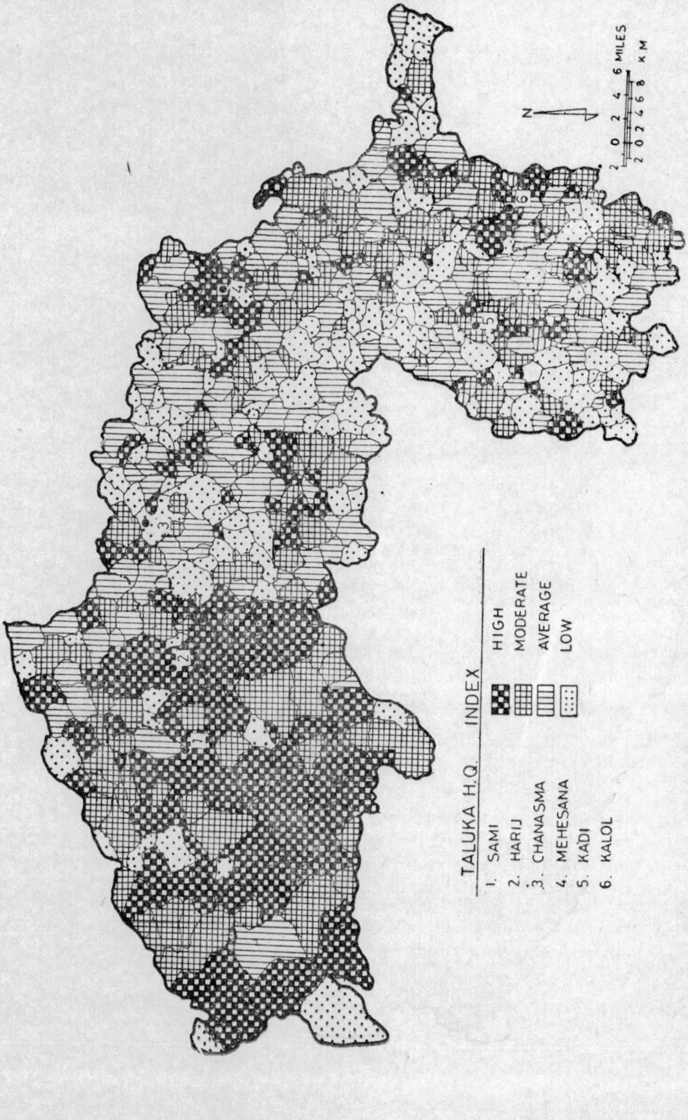

MAP 4.11: *Growth rate of population (1971-81) with respect to the study area*

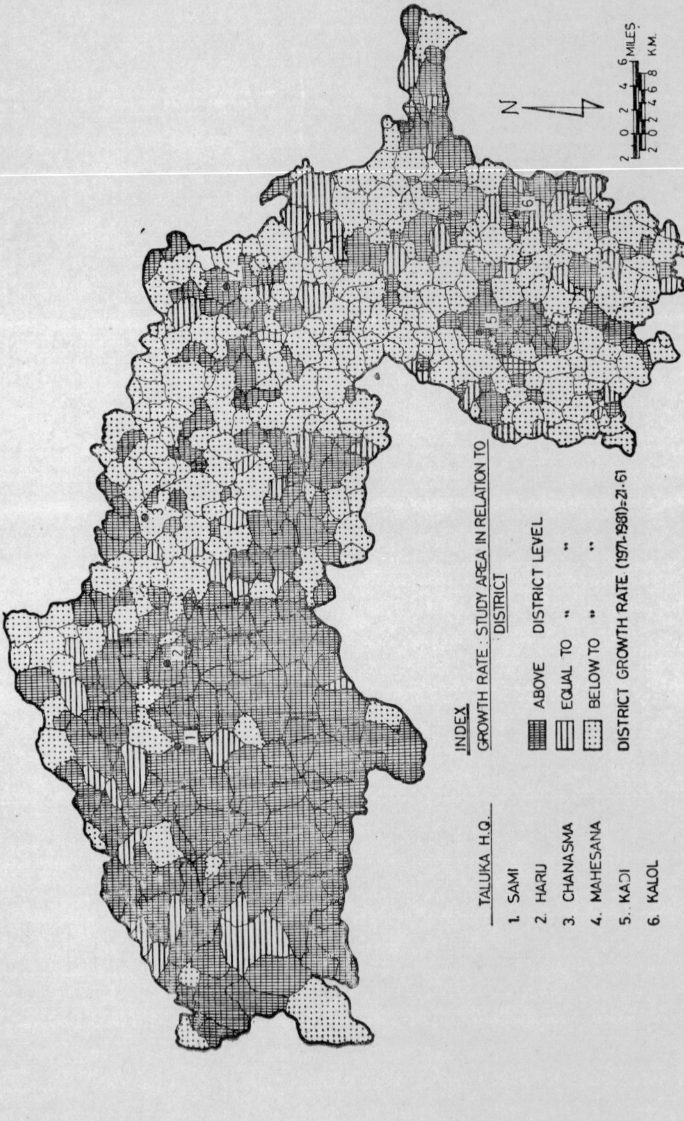

MAP 4.12: *Growth rate: Study area versus district*

that comparison (Map 4.12): the growth rate is unexpectedly high in the region of Sami taluka, parts of Harij and Chanasma talukas; the growth rate is lower than that of the district in northern Chanasma taluka, south-western Mahesana taluka, Kadi taluka and the north-eastern part of Kalol taluka; the growth rate has shown a negative correlation with the size of settlements, that is, smaller the size the higher the rate of growth. The relation is negative, and it is not significant to accept it as a hypothesis.

COMPOSITION

Composition of population like sex-ratio, literacy or work-participation rate indicate indirectly the quality of population. Female literacy is very low in Sami taluka followed by Harij (Table 4.6). The percentage is relatively high in Chanasma, Mahesana and Kalol areas. Total literacy as well as female literacy have increased in all talukas over a period of time (1951-1981). In general, urban literacy is higher (60 per cent) than that of rural literacy (45 per cent) in 1981. Female literacy has improved in the last two decades (27 per cent in 1971 and 35 per cent in 1981) compared to that in the previous decades (15 per cent in 1951 and 21 per cent in 1961).

TABLE 4.6 : **Literacy rate (1961-1981)**

(in percentage)

Taluka	1951		1961		1971		1981 (estimated)	
	Total	Female	Total	Female	Total	Female	Total	Female
Sami	6	2	12	4	16	6	23	11
Harij	13	6	19	9	22	12	29	17
Chanasma	24	14	35	23	40	28	48	35
Mahesana	27	16	36	23	43	31	52	42
Kadi	26	15	36	23	41	29	49	37
Kalol	26	17	36	23	41	30	49	37

Source : *District Census Handbook*, 1951, 1961 and 1971.

Age structure is helpful to understand the growth rate of population. Age structure is not available for taluka or village in the census of 1971 or 1981. However, in the 1961 census, Sami and Harij talukas had 44 per cent of the population below the age of 14 years, indicating its relation with high growth rate. On an average the same age group was lower (41 per cent) in other talukas.

Sex-ratio indicates indirectly the flow of indor out-migration. Sex-ratio (female per 1,000 males) is seen to be lower in urban areas (924 in 1981) compared to that in rural areas (954 in 1981) of the study area. Sami has shown an increasing sex-ratio since 1961 (930,956). Chanasma and Harij had the same trend, while Mahesana, Kadi and Kalol had a decrease in sex-ratio in 1971 from 1961, but increased again in 1981. An association of low sex-ratio and high non-primary workers is seen in this area; the percentage of female is high in the rural area, with higher agricultural activities while it is lower in the urban areas with higher non-primary activities. The percentage of female workers to total female population is low in Sami and Harij talukas while female participation is higher in Mahesana, Chanasma and Kalol talukas (Table 5.3).

5

FACTORS RELATED TO THE GROWTH AND DECLINE OF POPULATION

THIS chapter attempts to analyse the processes that have given rise to a system of settlements with certain demographic characteristics in the study area. There can be no exclusive answer to any system which involves complex and multi-faceted processes. As a result, an approach of complementarity has been stressed here to summarize and explain the manner in which settlements have grown or declined in terms of total population, density and growth rate of population. However, all aspects of demography can only be inferred as data on birth and death rates, in and out-migration, age-sex distribution by village are not available, as indicated earlier. Initially, various factors and their impact on the demographic aspects of settlements have been analysed and finally a classification of settlements, based on demographic and socio-economic characteristics, has been attempted in the following chapter.

PHYSICAL FACTORS

The study area varies from the west to the east—not so much from the point of view to topography but from the point of view of distribution of average annual rainfall and content of salinity and alkali in the soil. These physical factors are associated with demographic variables, especially with density, distribution of population and size of settlements. Though detailed rainfall data for several stations are not available, a projected isohyet map of distribution of average annual rainfall of 30 years is helpful (Map 5.1). In the west,

Average Annual Rainfall (in-cm)

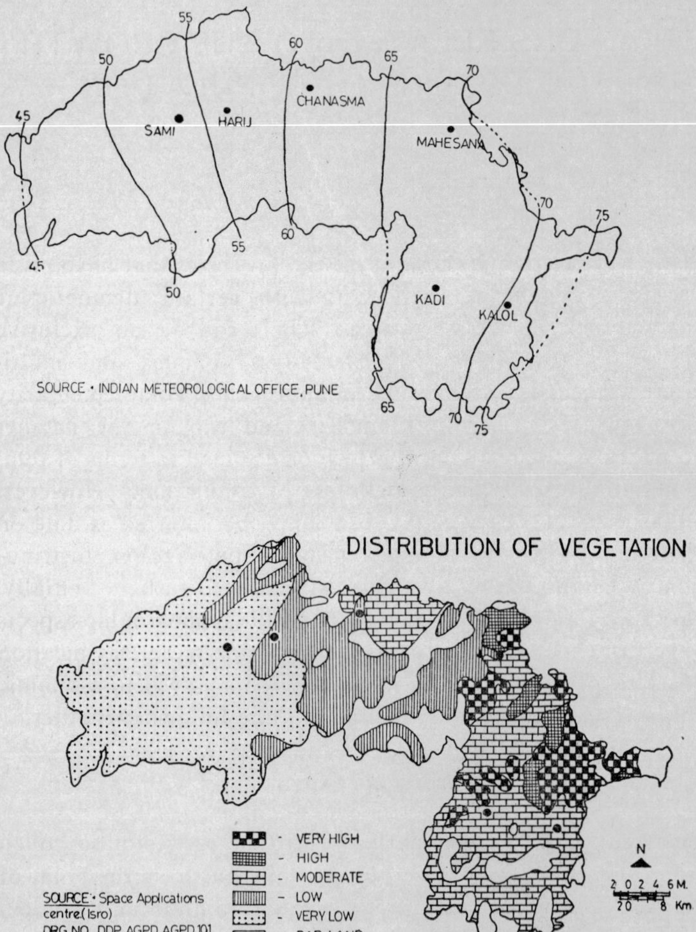

MAP 5.1: *Average annual rainfals and vegetation*

Sami taluka has a low rainfall of 45 cm. An association of rural density and the average density of population increases from the west to the east, so does the average annual rainfall. Besides density, low rainfall is also associated with low distribution of population and small size of settlements in this area. The situation is reverse where rainfall is higher in the eastern section (Maps 4.1, 4.2, 4.3, and 4.4). But the distribution of rainfall does not show much relationship with the growth rate of population. It is very random—both high and low growth rates are visible in dry and wet areas (Maps 4.7, 4.8, 4.9 and 4.11). Surprisingly, when the growth rate is compared to that of the district, Sami has indicated a higher growth rate than that of the district (Map 4.12); that may be related to cultural factors. Another physical determinant appears to be the nature of soil. Vegetation cover is a good reflector of rainfall and soil (Map 5.1). In the western side, in Sami and Harij areas, soil is saline and alkaline type with scanty vegetation (Map 5.2). Both density and distribution of population are low, while it is much higher in Mahesana and Kalol areas with calcareous, sandy to loamy soil with higher cropping intensity due to irrigation facilities.

ECONOMIC FACTORS

The impact of economic factors on the demograhpic aspects of settlements has been categorized into the following major divisions: (a) general socio-economic profile of the study area, and (b) occupational structure. An attempt here is made to have an idea of the general socio-economic background by taluka over a period of time.

General socio-economic profile

An overall condition of talukas, if not by villages, can be obtained on education, medical facilities, transport and communication of rural settlements in 1981 (Tables 5.1(a),(b).) The majority of villages have primary schools, but many of them do not have non-primary educational institutions or educational institutions of a higher level. The percentage of villages with higher secondary schools is low in Sami and Harij talukas, indicating a lower level of educational facilities

Distribution of Soil Salinity

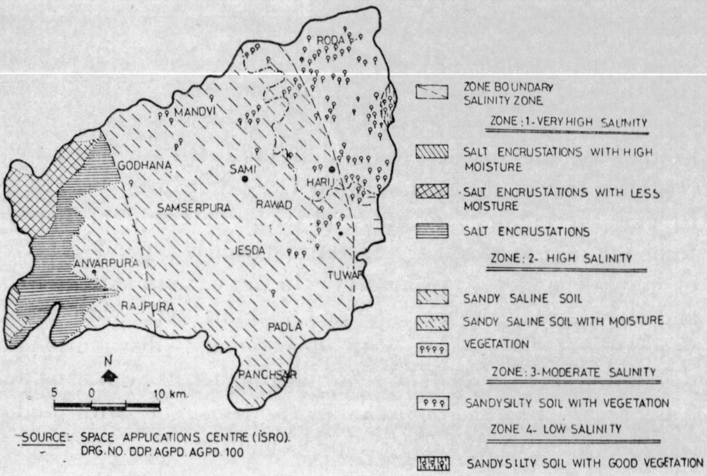

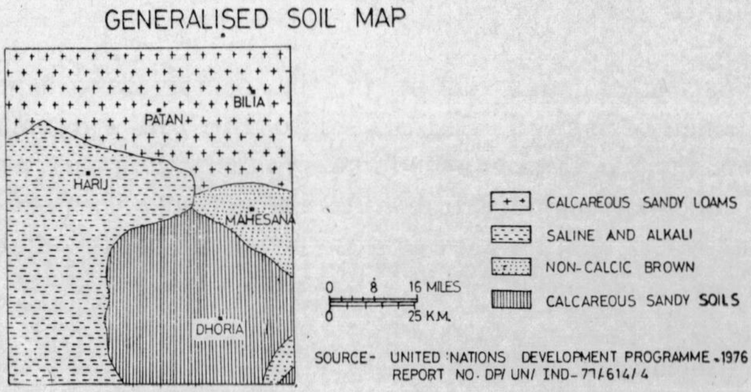

MAP 5.2: *Distribution of soil salinity and generalised soil map*

in the western side compared to that in the eastern section. This is reflected in the literacy of total as well as female population too. In terms of medical facilities, Sami has the

TABLE 5.1(a) : **Socio-economic profile of the study area (1981)**

Taluka	Total No. of villages	Non-primary educational institutions		Literacy		Medical institutions	
		No.	per cent	Total	Female	No.	per cent
Sami	97	15	15.5	23.37	10.69	39	40.2
Harij	39	4	10.2	24.51	12.44	23	58.9
Chanasma	110	50	45.0	46.28	33.61	79	71.2
Mahesana	109	38	34.9	48.84	36.39	93	85.3
Kadi	117	32	27.3	47.08	34.28	105	89.7
Kalol	68	36	38.2	44.87	31.92	40	59.0
Total Ave.	540	165	30.4	41.77	26.55	379	69.96

N.B.: Per cent in terms of taluka total.

TABLE 5.1 (b)

Taluka	Registered medical practitioners		Achievement in Family Planning	Per cent of villages with				
	No.	per cent	per cent	Metalled road	Railway station	Post offices	Phone connections	Agricultural and non-agro-electricity
Sami	11	11.23	20.13	27.8	—	45.4	10.3	21.6
Harij	7	17.9	39.41	33.3	—	43.6	5.1	79.5
Chanasma	26	23.6	40.99	33.3	9.9	49.5	26.1	93.7
Mahesana	64	58.7	60.54	39.4	16.5	50.4	56.9	100.0
Kadi	80	67.8	50.59	24.8	5.1	44.4	44.4	88.9
Kalol	40	58.8	59.81	42.6	8.82	67.6	35.3	83.8
Total Ave.	228	42.07	45.24	32.84	7.56	49.63	33.02	78.78

Note : Rural settlements have been considered here for 1981. Towns are not included in this table.

Source : Town Planning Office, Ahmedabad.

lowest percentage of villages having health services, and a large number of people (12,200 persons per bed) is served by a few public health centres. The situation is much better in the eastern section. The situation is the same for the distribution of registered medical practitioners, that is, few practitioners are in Sami compared to the east. The overall achievement in family planning is the lowest in Sami taluka, followed by Harij and Chanasma. The high growth of population in Sami can perhaps be attributed to the low rate of achievement in family planning. The situation is better in Mahesana, Kalol and Kadi talukas. In terms of transport and communication, only 27 per cent of villages in Sami has metalled roads. The condition of Kadi is worse. However, the condition is better in Mahesana and Kalol talukas. Many villages in the Sami area do not have all-year bus services (Map 5.7) due to unmetalled roads, and thus villages get disconnected in the rainy season. There is no railway station in Sami and Harij talukas. But villages in Kalol taluka have a better facility of post offices compared to Sami, Harij and Kadi talukas. The number of phones is also low in Sami and Harij talukas. The availability of electricity for agricultural or other purposes is low in the Sami-Harij area compared to the eastern side.

The table on the economic profile gives an overall impression of some aspects of economic conditions of the study area. The picture would have been clearer if the data on income, expenditure, savings, total production and yield per acre were available. In general, the western talukas, Sami and Harij, are relatively poor in terms of education and medical facilities, transport and communication, and electricity facilities. The situation is much better in Mahesana and Kalol talukas, while it is in an intermediate condition in Chanasma and Kadi talukas.

Occupational pattern

The occupational pattern by taluka (rural and urban) is an indirect indicator of economic condition of an area. In a balanced economy, the distribution of workers is proportionally divided between primary and other sectors of economy. The proportion of primary workers is very high in

Sami taluka (nearly 88 per cent), followed by Harij and and Chanasma (80 per cent), indicating a high dependence of population on one sector of economy, whereas Kalol and Mahesana have a more balanced economy by sector, having a larger proportion of workers in non-primary activity (Map 5.3). The Location Quotient value of non-primary workers by taluka (both for rural and urban settlements) is the highest in Kalol, followed by Mahesana and Kadi (Table 5.2). The Location Quotient value of raral non-primary workers is similarly the highest in Kalol, followed by Mahesana. It is the lowest in Sami followed by Harij and Chanasma, indicating the share of non-primary workers to total workers is lower in these talukas compared to that in the whole district. A further break-up of non-primary workers on a spatial distribution map clearly brings out that the north-eastern section of the study area has more non-primary workers than the western and southern sections of the

TABLE 5.2 : **Location quotient of non-primary workers (1971)**

Taluka	Percentage of non-primary workers to total worker	Percentage of rural non-primary workers to rural total workers	Total workers	Location Quotient* of non-primary workers (both rural and urban)	Location-Quotient** of non-primary workers (rural only)
Sami	12.20	12.00	28562	0.43	.70
Harij	19.80	8.53	17166	0.70	.42
Chanasma	19.70	19.46	47423	0.70	1.00
Mahesana	34.30	22.48	68625	1.22	1.23
Kadi	25.90	18.54	50715	0.92	.94
Kalol	42.40	24.52	48716	1.50	1.29
Total (study area)	28.20	71.80	261207		

*L.Q. : Non-primary workers of a taluka; Total workers of a taluka; Non-primary workers of the district; Total workers of the district.

**L.Q. : Rural non-primary workers of a taluka; Total rural workers of a taluka; Rural non-primary workers of the district; Total rural workers of the district.

Source : *District Census Handbook of Gujarat*, 1971.

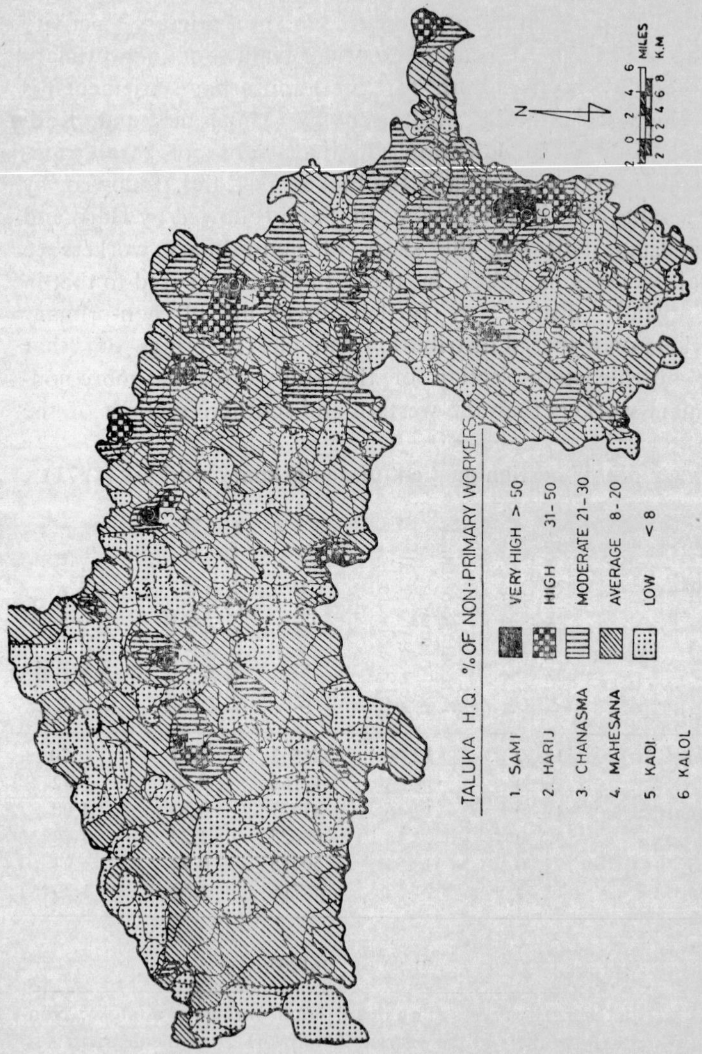

MAP 5.3: *Distribution of non-primary workers (1971)*

study area (Map 5.3 and Table 5.2). If the Location Quotient of non-primary workers of only rural settlements is considered (540 villages out of 546), some changes are noticeable (Table 5.2). Kalol town has a large number of jobs in non-primary activities. When the figure of Kalol town is removed from the L.Q. value has reduced. The situation is the same in Harij taluka. The impact of Mahesana town on its rural Location Quotient is not so high, suggesting the existence of non-primary occupation in villages of Mahesana taluka. Kadi taluka too has the same Location Quotient without the impact of Kadi town. The Location Quotient for the rural non-primary occupation has increased for Sami and Chanasma, perhaps for two large villages, that is, Sami itself and Dhinoj. Sami has the rural status, but as a taluka headquarters it is the centre of non-primary activities. As a result, when only the Location Quotient for rural workers engaged in non-primary activity is considered, the relative position of Sami has increased. Dhinoj, in Chanasma, has turned rural from urban in 1971. In spite of this change, Dhinoj still is a large village with people engaged in non-primary occupations. As a result of Dhinoj being added to the rural settlement, the Location Quotient of Chanasma has been increased.

In order to distinguish the dominant non-primary occupation of settlements, 50 per cent has been considered as the cut-off line. If a village is having more than 50 per cent of tertiary or secondary workers as a percentage of non-primary workers, the village is considered, here, having dominantly tertiary workers or dominantly secondary workers. The study area is mainly oriented to tertiary occupation (Map 5.4). The number of villages with mainly secondary type of non-primary occupation is seen in Kalol, Kadi and Mahesana and some in Sami areas. Both Harij and Chanasma have mainly tertiary type of non-primary occupation. All taluka headquarters are also oriented to the tertiary type of occupation. The secondary occupation, or industrial activity, is concentrated in the eastern section near the highway and railway line for connectivity, so that raw materials and finished products can be easily transported. In contrast, the majority of villages in the study area as a whole have trade, commerce or construction work other than primary occupation.

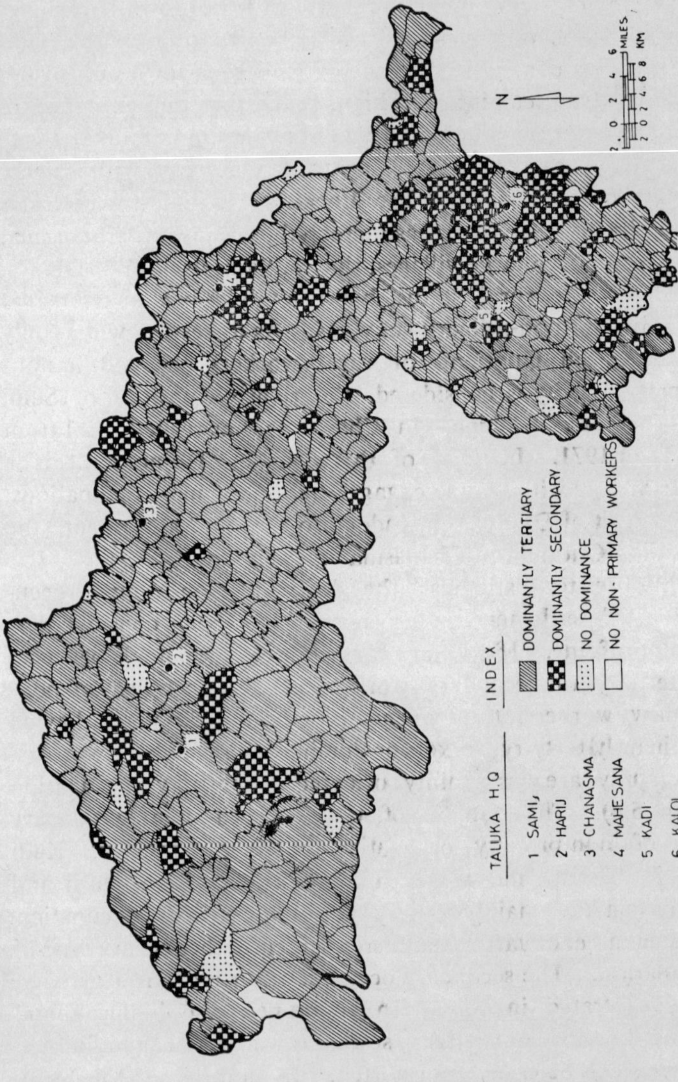

MAP 5.4: *Dominant non-primary workers (1971)*

There is not much variation by taluka in terms of percentage of workers. The percentage of workers is 28.57 per cent for the study area in 1971. The same holds good for percentage distribution of cultivators and agricultural labour. In the study area 64.7 per cent is cultivators and 35.3 per cent is agricultural labour of the total agricultural workers.

In general, the percentage of female workers to total female population is rather low in the study area (Table 5.3), indicating a low rate of participation, especially in the Sami area. Of the total, 43 per cent settlements only had less than 3 per cent as female workers in the study area.

TABLE 5.3 : **Female workers to total female population (1971)**

Taluka	Low	Average	Moderate	High	Total
Value in per cent	3 per cent	3.1-9 per cent	9.1-12 per cent	12 per cent	Total villages
Sami	49	27	6	15	97
Harij	16	9	5	10	40
Chanasma	49	39	5	19	112
Mahesana	39	43	12	16	110
Kadi	54	47	9	8	118
Kalol	28	27	4	10	69
Total	235	192	41	78	546

Source: District Census Handbook of Gujarat, 1971.

IRRIGATION, CROP PATTERN AND LAND USE

The study area has experienced an increase in the total irrigated land during 1961-1962 to 1977-1978 (Table 5.4). The total irrigated land has increased from 58,550 hectares to 109,371 hectares. The rate of increase of irrigated area to gross cropped area is mainly noticeable in Mahesana and Kalol followed by Chanasma, Kadi, Harij and Sami during 1961-62 to 1977-78 (Table 5.4). The overall situation is not so bright in the western side, in terms of irrigation, especially in Sami taluka (Map 5.5).

In the study area, data on irrigation was available by village for Kalol taluka in 1981 (Table 5.5 and Fig. 5.1). The number of villages having low irrigation has decreased while it has increased in villages with high percentage of irrigation

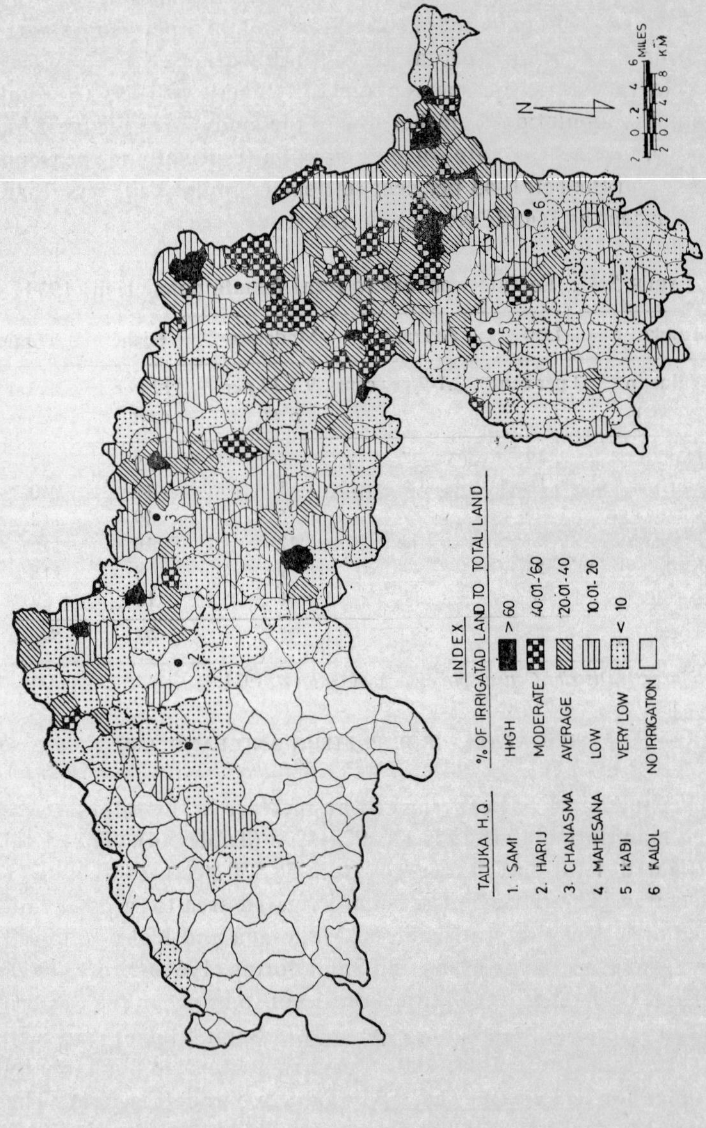

MAP 5.5: *Irrigated area (1971)*

TABLE 5.4 : **Pattern of irrigation (1961-1978)**

Taluka	Total irrigated land (in hectare)		Per cent of irrigated Area to gross cropped area	
	1961-62	1977-78	1961-62	1977-78
Sami	1335	2007	2.04	2.00
Harij	2517	7390	7.40	21.48
Chanasma	7452	16131	10.05	22.12
Mahesana	15574	35408	21.70	44.90
Kadi	17135	26600	24.30	33.50
Kalol	14537	21775	23.30	45.00
Total	58550	109371		

Source : Directorate of Agriculture, Government of Gujarat.

TABLE 5.5 : **The pie-diagram for (Kalol taluka) on irrigated**

Categories of irrigated land	Per cent of irrigated land to total land	No. of villages 1971	No. of villages 1981	Degree in pie 1971	Degree in pie 1981
Low irrigation	0 to 15 per cent	37	19	195	101
Average irrigation	15.01 to 40 per cent	24	18	127	95
Moderate irrigation	40.01 to 60 per cent	4	19	21	100
High irrigation	> 60 per cent	3	12	16	64
Total		68	68	360°	360°

Percentage of mean irrigated area to total Area in Kalol } 1971 X = 18.80; 1981 X = 37.47

Source : District Census Handbook 1971 and taluka headquarter's office.

during 1971-1981 in Kalol. A composite pie-diagram, with circles of areas proportional to the irrigated areas of 1971 and 1981, has been prepared. The four sections in each circle represent the four classes of irrigation level, i.e. high, moderate, average and low. The percentages of villages of these four classes have been depicted as angles of sectors, i.e. 100 per cent representing as 360°.

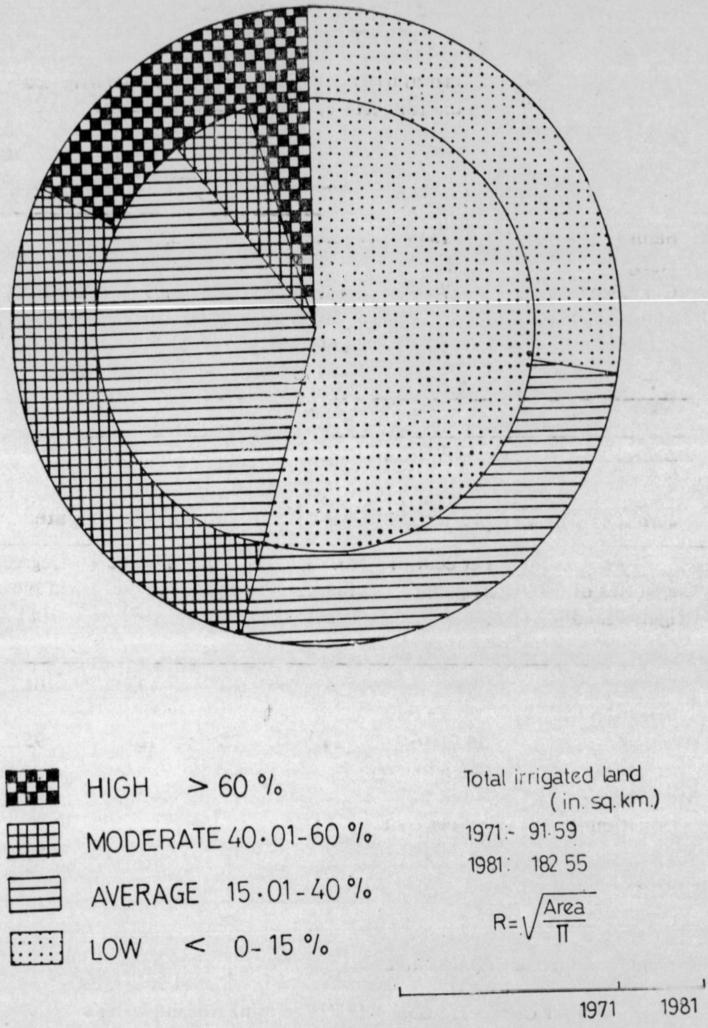

FIG. 5.1: *Pie-diagram showing the percentage of irrigated land in Kalol taluka (1971 & 1981)*

The impact of irrigation is seen on cropping intensity and land use efficiency of an area (Tables 5.6 (a)(b)). In the study area, the cultivable land (during 1975-76 to 1977-78) does not vary much by taluka. Sami has increased its cultivable area by 5 per cent during 1968-69 to 1970-71 to 1975-76 to 1977-78. There has been a slight decrease in the case of Mahesana, while

TABLE 5.6 (a) : **Land use pattern (1968-1978)**

Name of taluka	Total area in hectare 1975-76 to 1977-78	Cultivable Area (per cent)		Per cent of net sown area to cultivable area	
		1968-69 to 1970-71	1975-76 to 1977-78	1968-69 to 1970-71	1975-76 to 1977-78
Sami	150986	83.11	88.75	68.87	77.04
Harij	40700	85.33	85.72	85.25	88.24
Chanasma	89372	84.54	84.39	95.58	90.82
Mahesana	79038	87.46	86.19	95.80	97.66
Kadi	83169	86.91	86.73	94.56	94.08
Kalol	48728	86.94	88.37	95.07	91.72

TABLE 5.6 (b)

Name of taluka	Gross gropped area (per cent)		Cropping intensity		Average land use efficiency
	1968-69 to 1970-71	1975-76 to 1977-78	1968-69 to 1970-71	1975-76 to 1977-78	1968-78
Sami	57.43	73.80	100	107	66.89
Harij	77.97	84.54	107	111	85.93
Chanasma	85.36	81.58	105	106	93.23
Mahesana	101.31	100.36	120	119	96.60
Kadi	90.89	93.63	110	114	94.73
Kalol	96.69	98.57	117	121	91.61

$$\text{Cropping intensity} = \frac{\text{Gross cropped area}}{\text{Net Sown area}} \times 100$$

$$\text{Land use efficiency} = \frac{\text{Net sown area}}{\text{Cultivable area}} \times 100$$

Source : Directorate of Agriculture, Government of Gujarat.

other talukas have remained the same in percentage. But the variation is visible in terms of net sown area to cultivable area. The percentage of net sown area is lowest in Sami whereas it is much higher in the eastern taluka, but the rate of increase is highest in Sami during 1970-71 to 1977-78. Similarly, in terms of gross cropped area, cropping intensity and the average land use efficiency, the western side, especially Sami, is rather poor compared to that of the eastern side, with a higher percentage of irrigation. But the rate of increase in gross cropped area and cropping intensity is high in the western section of Sami area. Of course, the vital data of yield per acre, if available, would have been much more meaningful to bring out the impact of irrigation on land use pattern.

The impact of irrigation can be analysed over time and space, that is, the first period in the beginning of irrigation (1965-1968) and the second period after 10 years of irrigation (1975-1978). The areas with a higher percentage of irrigation are mainly located in Mahesana and Kalol, and those with low percentage of irrigation are in Sami and Harij talukas (Table 5.4). The analysis focuses on changes mainly on five crops, that is, Bajri, wheat, condiments, cotton and fodder (Appendix III).

During the first and the second period, the mean area under Bajri has much increased while that under wheat has slightly decreased. The per cent share of irrigated land under Bajri has similarly increased while it has decreased under wheat. But the overall irrigated land used for wheat is much higher (21 per cent in 1975-1978) compared to that of Bajri (6 per cent). The increase of irrigated land used for Bajri is mainly seen in Kalol, Mahesana and Kadi. The irrigated land for wheat has increased in Kalol while it has decreased in Mahesana and Kadi. In the western side, the irrigated land for wheat has decreased in Sami but it has increased in Harij and Chanasma talukas during 1975-1978. Condiments have increased both on highly irrigated lands of Mahesana and on lowly irrigated areas of Sami and Harij. The overall production of condiments has increased much in the second period. There has been an increase in cotton areas especially in Mahesana, Kadi and Kalol and the same with fodder crops which have increased mainly in Chanasma, Kadi and Mahesana. In short, there has been an increase of irrigated land for Bajri, condiments and fodder crops and decrease in wheat and cotton, though these two crops occupy still the large share of irrigated lands.

Finally, it is worth while to note the impact of irrigation on the total population, density of population and the growth rate of population. Taking two extreme talukas—Sami, which has a low percentage of irrigated land, and Kalol, which has a high percentage of irrigated land—it is seen that relationship is significant between per cent irrigated land with density and total population but, there is not much relationship with the growth rate of population (Table 5.7).

TABLE 5.7 : **Irrigation versus population**
(Kalol and Sami Talukas)
1971—1981

Irrigation	Demographic factor	Chi-square Relation	Correlation
Per cent irrigated to total land (1981)	Density	Significant	.60
Total irrigated area (1971)	Totol Population (1971)	Significant	.82
Per cent change in irrigated land (1971-81)	Growth rate of population (1971-1981)	None	.011

N.B. : Significance level is 95 per cent.
Source : *District Census Handbook* and field work.

CONNECTIVITY AND RELATIVE LOCATION

Site and situation are two important factors for the growth and decline of settlements. The site of a settlement remains static in absolute terms, but it becomes dynamic in the relative sense when its connectivity is increased to other settlements and areas. Here relative location has been used in the sense of situation, referring to the location of a settlement with respect to location of other settlements. In this study, the relative location of a settlement has been analysed in terms of physical distance from the taluka headquarters, district headquarters, railway station and nearest town. Geographical distance changes over time as connectivity brings settlements closer to each other. Connectivity, on the other hand, will be created if there is a need for settlements to interact. By summing the distance of each settlement from the abovementioned variables, weightage is given for relative location. The relative location is high in the north and eastern section with very high values around taluka headquarters (Map 5.6). Kadi and Kalol areas have been joined in a linear fashion towards an external pull of Ahmedabad in the south-east;

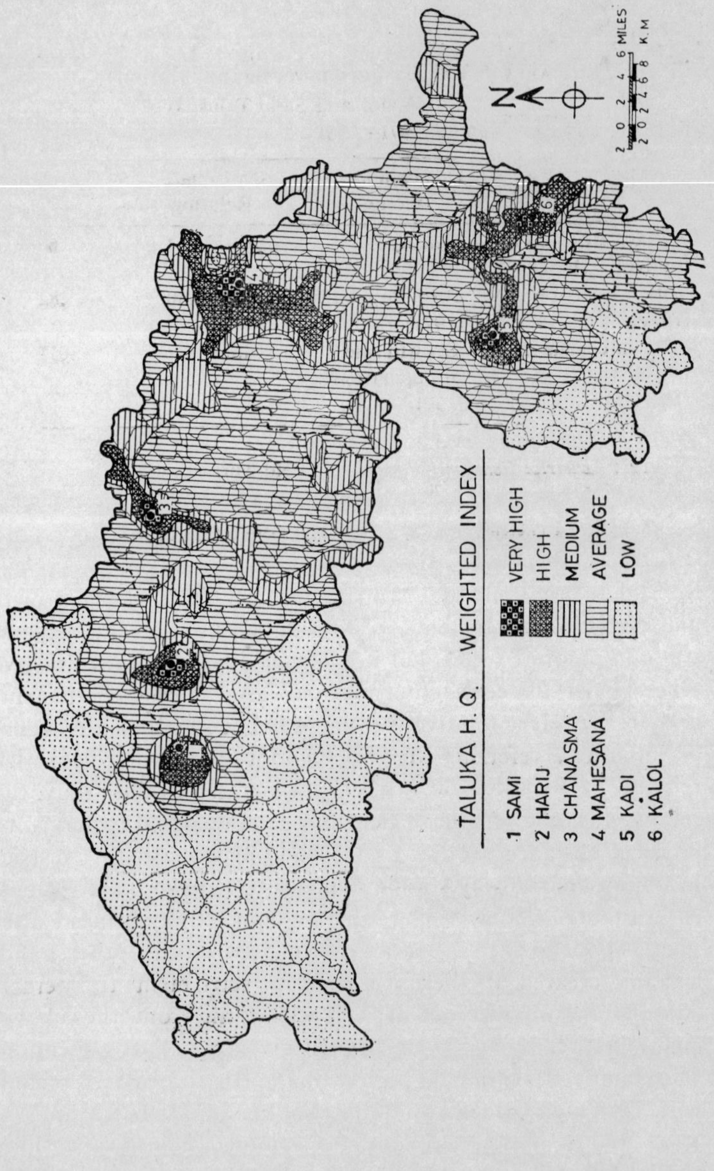

MAP 5.6: *Relative location of settlement (1971)*

similarly Mahesana has an external pull of Unjha, and Chanasma has it towards Patan. Sami area and southern Kadi show a low level of relative location.

As location is very much related to connectivity, a somewhat similar trend is visible in Map 5.7 dealing with it. Connectivity here includes type of roads (metalled and unmetalled) and type of bus service (all-weather and fair weather) in each village. A flow map of frequency of State Transport buses in the study area brings out clearly the hierarchical pattern of nodes and the system of interaction of passengers everyday (Map 5.8). The flow map depicts Kalol as the highest node though Mahesana is the district headquarters. The frequency of buses is the highest in Kalol as it is closer to Ahmedabad, followed by Mahesana and Kadi. Dhinoj in the north and Bechraji in the south of Chanasma taluka come next in the hierarchy. Bechraji, being a religious and trade centre, has high connectivity and high frequency of buses. As a result of high connectivity, Bechraji has thrived in economic activities. It has become an important marketing sub-yard and it gained the status of a town in 1981, with more than 75 per cent male workers engaged in non-primary occupations (as one of the factors of its township). As relative location and general connectivity are poor in Sami and Harij talukas, same is true for frequency of buses. In this area, many villages have only one bus service during the day; some do not have even that and some are having bus services only in the fair seasons. The majority of roads, in this western side, are unmetalled and remain waterlogged during the rainy season, when all these villages get totally isolated from the rest of the region. As a result, all types of socio-economic interactions come to a standstill. Location and connectivity are the vital nerves of settlements that make accessible to villagers' employment, amenities and facilities around them. In general, total population and density of population have shown a fairly good correlation with connectivity "r" being .50 and .44 respectively.

AMENITIES, SHOPS AND ESTABLISHMENTS

In general, the existence of amenities, shops and establishments

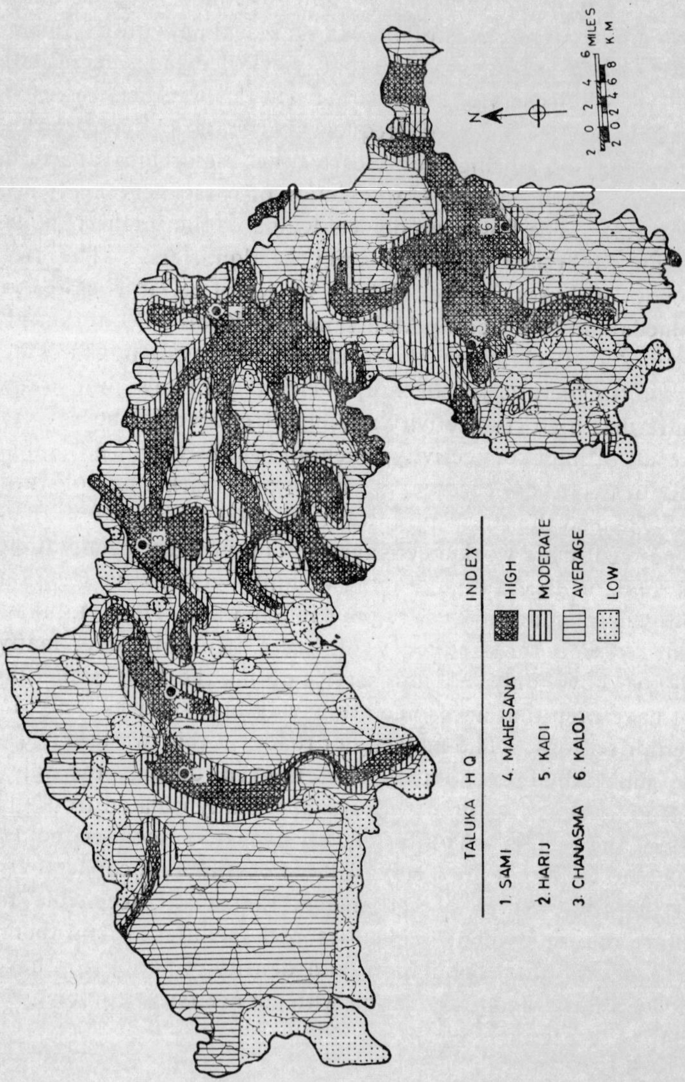

MAP 5.7: *Connectivity on space*

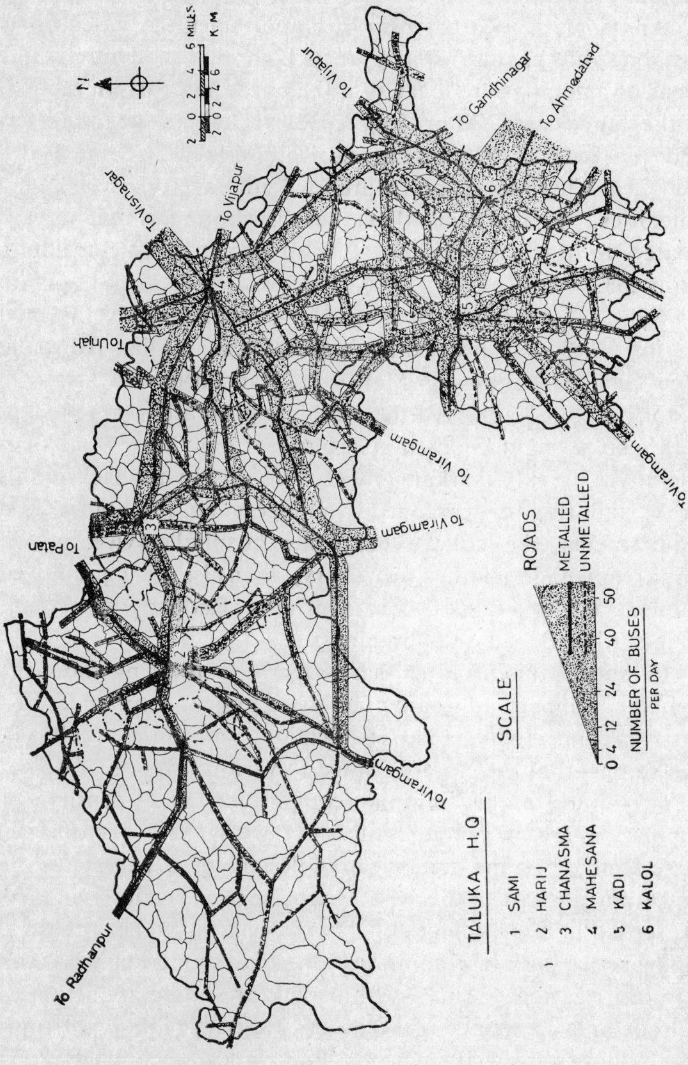

MAP 5.8: *Flow map of bus service (1981)*

can be associated with the size of population. Each is dependent on the other. It is an indicator of the economic health of a settlement, showing a diversified base of occupation and functions.

An isopleth map of distribution of amenities based on 30 variables brings out clearly that high and moderately high areas of amenities are located in the north and eastern sections of the study area (Map 5.9), covering taluka headquarters and in parts of Mahesana and Kalol talukas, Sami, Harij, southern Chanasma and southern Kadi have relatively fewer amenities. It is found that the distribution of amenities is related to the distribution of total population, correlation being .63.

Next to the taluka headquarters, secondary level of interaction takes place around Bechraji, Dhiroj, Jillia, Adiwada; Meu and Ambaliasan in Mahesana, Ranchorda and Jaspur in Kalol, Thol in Kadi. All these centres generally serve villages within six to eight kilometres in terms of daily needs, milk co-operatives, weekly market, grocery and provision, blacksmith's work, tailoring or carpentry. Villagers go for higher level requirements like college education, hospital service, market yard, readymade clothes, jewellery, utensils, or agricultural implements to taluka headquarters, Radhanpur, Patan, Unjha, Ahmedabad and Viramgam.

In short, this chapter has attempted to bring about the combined impact of many factors—physical, economic, irrigation, connectivity, relative location, amenities, cultural, and so on—that are closely related to various aspects of demography—its size, distribution, composition and density of population, are, in general, consistent with these factors. All these factors become quite clear while making a survey of the field from the east to the west. In the eastern section, villagers are settled in large villages or towns with a higher density. Villagers are busy in reaping two or even three crops with the help of irrigation. Along with agriculture, there are activities of trade and commerce and industry, offering job opportunities. Villages are well connected to have socio-economic interactions which are indicated in a high population potential. A combination of all these factors has obviously given rise to a system of settlement pattern—from large size, closely spaced

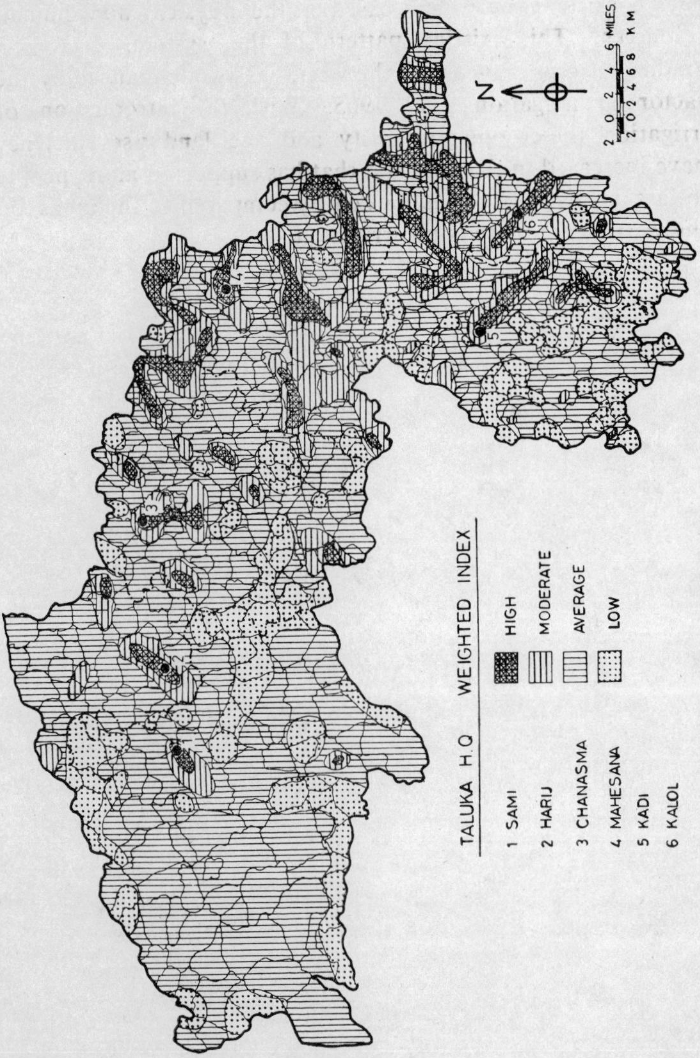

MAP 5.9: *Distribution of amenities (1971)*

with high density, high amenities, good connectivity and location in the east to a system of settlements with reverse situation in the west.

It is important to note that the pattern of settlements has been consistent since 1951, based on the physical and human resources. This existing pattern of the system, having a gradient from the east to the west, has been enhanced by the factor of irrigation since 1965. With the introduction of irrigation, the cropping intensity and the land use efficiency have increased in the east and that has supported more people in larger villages with higher density compared to the areas on the west where there is no irrigation.

6

SETTLEMENTS IN A SYSTEM

IT HAS been noticed so far that settlements essentially form a morphological pattern on space. And the processes that have been responsible to bring about such a form are being influenced by the form itself. Recognizing that time and space are inseparable, form and movements are highly interdependent, in the settlement system. This section attempts to classify the system that has emerged in this part of Gujarat into subsets for a meaningful generalization. The information on the system of functional and population hierarchy and on the development potentiality of such subsets is relevant as it identifies problem areas and spatial inequality. This knowledge is very much needed for planning so that factors or processes can be manipulated to bring about the structure that is desirable for society.

FUNCTIONAL VERSUS POPULATION HIERARCHY

Settlements have been grouped into six classes, combining functions and size of population. Here towns and villages with a population of more than 2,000 in 1971 have been considered, summing up to 119 settlements out of 546. A weighted score, based on scarcity principle (Appendix II) on some central functions, like education, medical, connectivity, post and telegraph, electricity and drinking water and non-primary occupation, has been allotted to each settlement and then log of rank and log of functional scores have been plotted (Fig. 6.1). Distinct breaks are seen in the graph which are used for functional classification. In the first

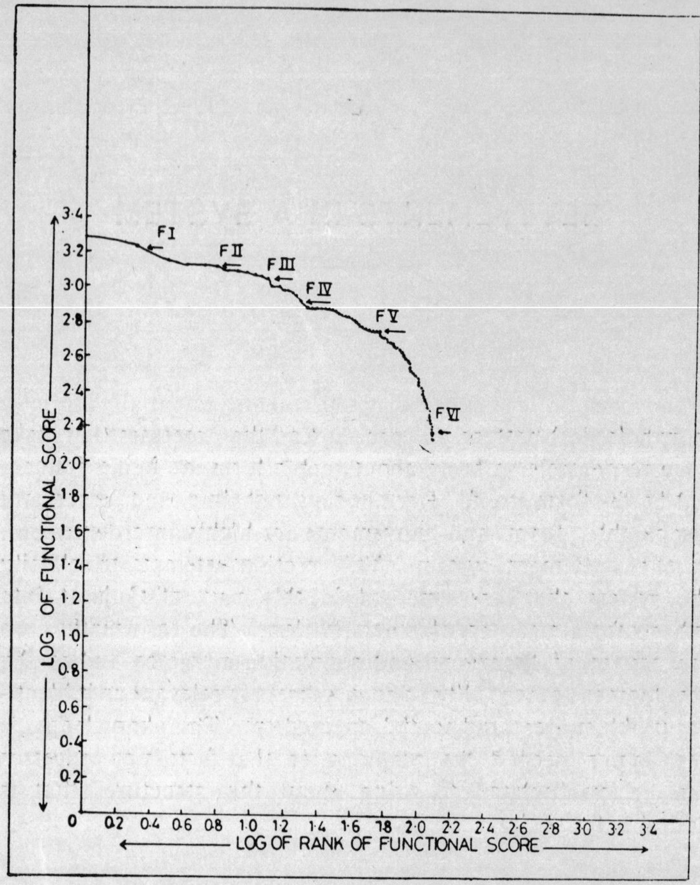

FIG. 6.1: *Functional hierarchy (1971)*

group, F I, Mahesana ranks first in functional score, followed closely by Kalol town. A sharp break is marked after Kalol. The second category (F II) includes Kadi town, Dhinoj, Harij, town and Chanasma town. This is followed by a small break including a number of villages like Jagudan, Nardipur, Langhnaj, Jotana, Bechraji and Sami to form the F III group. Another small break after this is followed by a somewhat steeper break with a series of villages, forming F IV group. One more break is traceable for the F V group, then the curve goes down in a round manner to include the rest of the settlements in F VI group.

In the other graph, the same 119 settlements have been ranked by population and are plotted to group them into population classes P I to P VI in relation to the breaks obtained in the graph (Fig. 6.2). An ideal line of rank-size rule distribution as per $p_n = p_1/n$ is also drawn for a comparison with the actual line of size-distribution. As in the functional

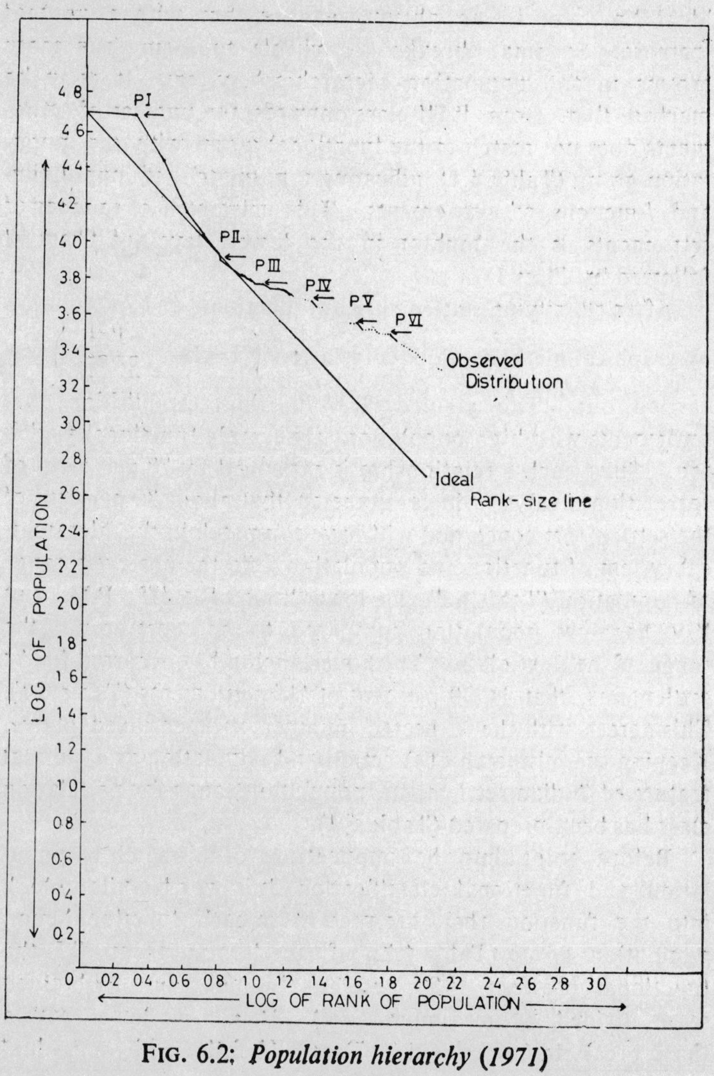

FIG. 6.2: *Population hierarchy (1971)*

group F I, Mahesana town ranks first also in population group P I, followed closely by Kalol town, forming a plateau. Then a sharp break is seen with the same four settlements of Kadi town, Dhinoj, Harij town and Chanasma town forming the P II group. This P II group meets the ideal line with a break for the next group to start. From this point, the observed line of distribution again goes above the expected ideal line, not in an abrupt manner, but with a gradual increase. So small breaks are visible to form four more groups in the population hierarchical system. It is to be marked that, from P III class onwards, the number of settlements does not match in the functional group with the population group (Table 6.1) indicating a mismatch of population and functions of settlements. This mismatch of number of settlements is the highest in the lowest level of Class VI followed by Class IV.

After classifying settlements by functions and population by graphical methods, rank-correlation $\left(r=1-\frac{6\Sigma d^2}{n^3-n} \right)$ was carried out. This yielded R=.70, thus establishing that settlements with high populations are largely functionally rich too. Since such a relationship is explained by 70 per cent of correlation analysis, it is expected that about 30 per cent of the settlements concerned will have mismatch in the hierarchical system of function and population. In the observed range of population (Table 6.2), the lower limit of P III, P IV and P V has low population compared to the upper limit of the range of the next class. Thus overlapping has occurred for 34 settlements, that is, 30 per cent of 119 settlements (Table 6.1). This agrees with the expected number as mentioned above. Keeping the mismatch of function and population as a normal feature of Indian settlements, population range for population class has been prepared (Table 6.1).

Before going into the implications of mismatch of population and functional classification, it is worth while to look into the functions that are present in each functional-cum-population group (Table 6.2). In the largest group, F I, the functional presence is 90 per cent (i.e. per cent of obtained score divided by maximum score). It comes down, with a sharp break, to 66 per cent in Class F II, followed by a gradual

TABLE 6.1 : **Population versus functional hierarchy**

Functional group	Range of functional score	Settlement in functional group (No.)	Population group	Population range	Settlements in population group (No.)	Mismatch in hierarchy of population & function
F I	1709-1904	2	P I	30,000+	2	—
F II	1285-1429	4	P II	8,500—29,999	4	—
F III	1129-1232	6	P III	5,500—8,499	8	2
F IV	753-1004	18	P IV	4,500—5,499	7	11
F V	564-747	25	P V	3,500—4,499	19	6
F IV	137-538	64	P VI	2,000—3,499	79	—
Total		119			119	34

Rank correlation between population size and functional score=0.70
Functional and population range classifications are based on respective graphs (Figs. 11, 12).

TABLE 6.2 : **Functional classification of settlements**

Functional class	No. of settlements above 2000 population	Range of functional score	Observed range of population in functional class	Average functional presence	Functions available in settlements
(1)	(2)	(3)	(4)	(5)	(6)
F I	2	1709 to 1904	50300 to 51600	90 per cent	1) College, vocational training institutes 2) Family welfare centre, bigger hospital and other medical facilities 3) 88 per cent of non-primary workers to total workers, and all the lower-level functions.
F II	4	1285 to 1429	8400 to 27900	66 per cent	1) Some educational institutes other than ordinary schools 2) Small hospital 3) Railway station 4) Protected water supply 5) 68 per cent of non-primary workers, and all the functions of the

(1)	(2)	(3)	(4)	(5)	(6)
					lower functional classes.
F III	6	1129 to 1232	3600 to 6800	59 per cent	1) Whole year bu service 2) Post and telegraph, phone 3) 46 per cent non-primary workers, and all the functions of the lower functional classes.
F IV	18	753 to 1004	3000 to 7400	42 per cent	1) Electricity for all purposes 2) Metalled road 3) 27 per cent non-primary workers to total workers, and the following functions.
F V	25	564 to 747	2100 to 6400	31 per cent	1) Secondary school 2) Dispensary 3) Electricity (partial) 4) Tap for drinking water 5) 23 per cent non-primary workers to total workers, and the following functions.

TABLE 6.2. (*Contd.*)

(1)	(2)	(3)	(4)	(5)	(6)
F VI	64	137 to 538	2000 to 4800	18 per cent	1) Primary school 2) Unmetalled road 3) Fair season bus service 4) Well for drinking water 5) Post office, and 6) 18 per cent non-primary workers to total workers.

N.B. : Functional presence $= \frac{\text{Obtained score}}{\text{Maximum score}} \times 100$

Functions available : More than 50 per cent of the settlements having that function.

Source : *District Census Handbook* (1971).

decline of functional presence of 59 per cent in F III, 42 per cent in F IV, 31 per cent in F V and 18 per cent in F VI. Consequently, the range of functional score also decreases first at a sudden rate, then at a gradual rate. In the lowest functional class of F VI, the minimum functions available are primary school, unmetalled roads, fair-season bus service, wells for drinking water, post office facility and 18 per cent of non-primary workers. In F V group, all functions of F VI group are available along with a secondary school, dispensary, electricity for agricultural use, tap for drinking water and 23 per cent of non-primary workers. Group F IV has all the functions of F VI and F V and electricity for all purposes, metalled roads and 27 per cent of non-primary workers. All the functions of groups F VI, F V, F IV are included in F III along with round-the-year bus service, post, telegraph and telephone exchange and 46 per cent of non-primary workers. Group F II has all these functions stated above and also some educational institutions other than ordinary schools, small hospital, railway station, protected water supply and 68 per cent of non-primary workers. Group F I towns have all the above functions. Besides, they have a college, vocational training institutes, a family welfare centre, a large hospital and 88 per cent of non-primary workers to total workers.

The hierarchy of functions and population has been depicted in a composite map (Map 6.1). The map brings out settlements having a match of population group with functional group as well as one with mismatch of the two. In Sami taluka, settlements are of small size in P VI and they have fewer functions of F VI group. Taluka headquarters Sami has a higher population (P III) compared to its functions (F IV). No other taluka headquarters has such a mismatch. It is interesting to note that out of 34 mismatched settlements, 27 of them have higher functions compared to their population size. The majority of them are from P VI of population group with F V of functional group. Some are also with P V population group with F IV functional base. Among this trend, one is Bechraji, in Chanasma, which has a high function group of F III with a low population group of P V, possibly due to the religious and trade significance of the place.

This kind of mismatch of higher functional base with a

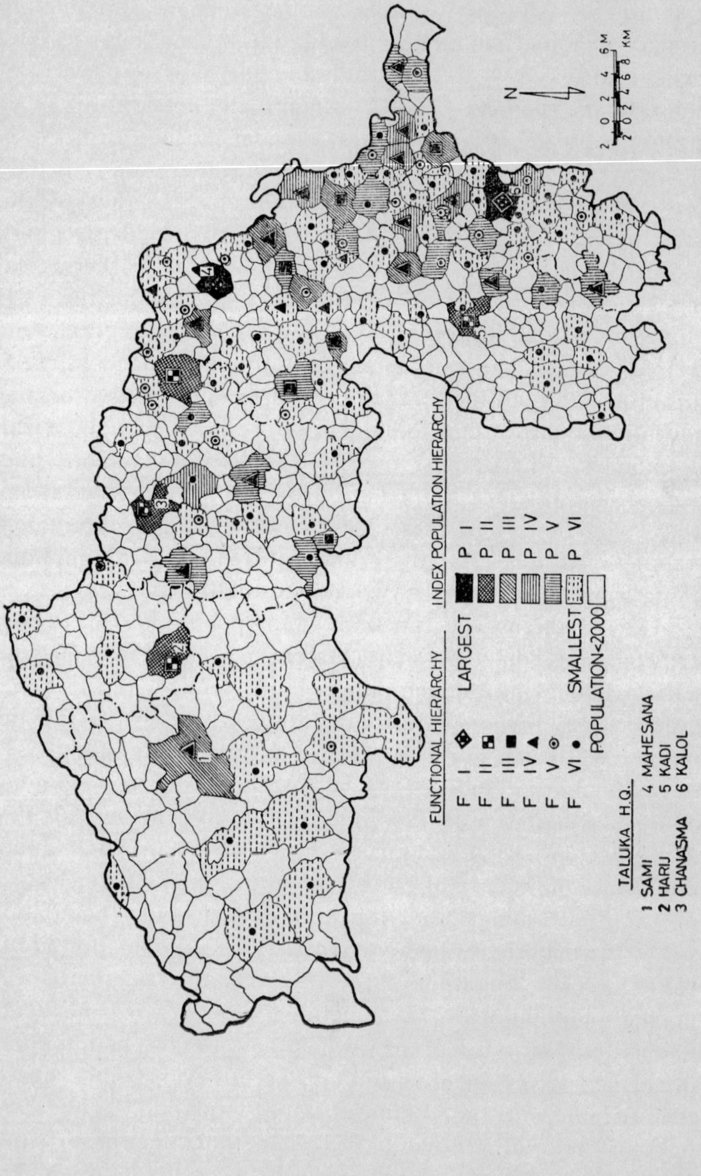

MAP 6.1: *Functional versus population hierarchy (1971)*

relatively lower population indicates a hopeful sign of rural development. Such villages are mainly seen in the northern part of Mahesana taluka, around Mahesana town, some are in the northern part of Chanasma and eastern Kalol. This may be due to the external economic impact of Unjha in the north and Ahmedabad and Gandhinagar in the south-east. It appears that villages are now having more infrastructural facilities than before. The implications of this aspect will be further discussed in the concluding chapter.

SETTLEMENT IN A SYSTEM OF DEVELOPMENT POTENTIAL

The meaning of "development" is not only very complex conceptually but also in terms of measurement and implementation. It is difficult to conceptualize "development" as it is relative and it changes over time and space. More so, if the changes are done very fast, say, switching from urban development programme to rural development one or agricultural development programme to industrial development one. Previously, prior to 1960, economic growth was considered as "development". Later, modernization, a process of social change in which economic growth is an important component, was considered "development". Since neither the growth pole theory was functioning for "spreading effect" to rural area, nor was the diffusion of knowledge or social change perculating from urban centres, so recently the concept of removal of spatial inequality came into being as a symbol of "development". It is advocated that there should be an even distribution and accessibility of goods and services to all regions. So several studies were carried out to find out the different levels of growth or developments by areas, type of problems by area, combining a number of indicators. Planning is then done accordingly. The minimum basic needs of villages are determined by the value judgements of the decision maker as well as availability of resources.

This study also makes an attempt to classify the villages into groups of "development potential", by combining a number of socio-economic weighted variables, e.g. total population, population potential, density and agricultural density, proportion of irrigated land, cultivated area, growth

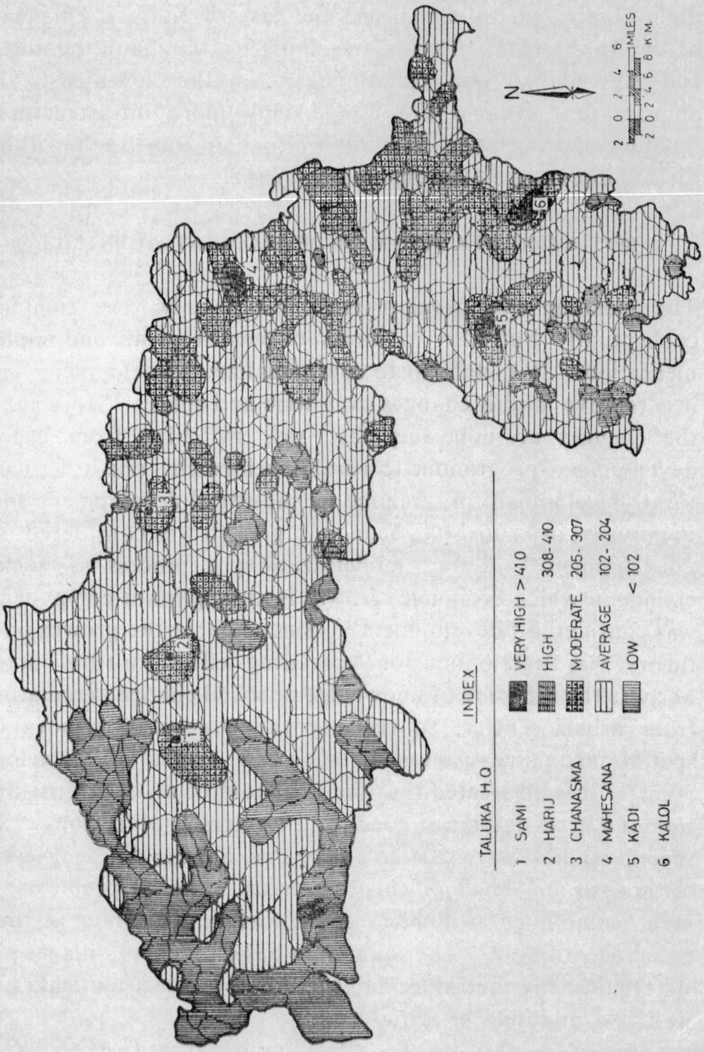

MAP 6.2: *Development potential (1971-1981)*

rate of population, proportions of female workers, percentage of female literacy, percentage of total workers, percentage of non-primary workers, amenities of 30 types, connectivity and flow of buses, relative location. Economic data on income, production, revenue, savings have not been used as these are not available on a village level for a quantitative assessment. As many of the variables are not taken up, this is not a comprehensive measurement of "development". However, it does give a general idea for understanding the potentiality for an area to develop (Map 6.2). The western section and south-western parts show low level of potentiality to develop, while it is higher in the north and eastern sections mostly around towns. The average potentiality for villages is the highest in Mahesana, followed by Kalol, Chanasma, Kadi, Harij and Sami. This is an expected result, as each of these above variables has indicated a similar pattern when analysed earlier in Chapter 5.

This exercise of grouping the villages into a hierarchical system and levels of development potential is not just to identify problem areas and developed areas. The issue is more critical—how to monitor the process of development ? Should it be from "top" starting from few development growth centres, or from "bottom" to the top ? It has been noticed that not villages are better off with more infrastructural facilities to have "place prosperity". Will the place prosperity bring automatically "people's prosperity" by bringing a convergence of life-style, income and social well-being between rural and urban areas ? Implications of these questions are far-reaching and can be decided by policy-makers.

7

SAMPLE VILLAGES AT A GLANCE

METHODOLOGY : SAMPLING AND ANALYSIS

IN Chapter 2 mention was made of the sampling technique of 53 villages out of 546 settlements in the study area (Map 7.1). Two types of villages have been selected—growing villages with constantly high, increasingly high and sudden growth rate of population during the last three decades (1951-1981), and declining villages with constantly low, decreasingly low and sudden fall in growth rate in the above period. All these villages had a minimum population of 500 in 1951 and are distributed in all six talukas. These villages have high or low percentage of irrigated land. They are located either near the Taluka Headquarters or away from them. Two special cases have been selected: Dhinoj and Bechraji in Chanasma taluka—Dhinoj turned from urban to rural in 1971 while Bechraji has become an urban settlement with a high percentage of non-primary workers.

The selected villages have been further classified into three groups based on the availability of irrigated land, so that the impact of irrigation on overall demographic aspects and development potential can be assessed (Appendix IV). The average percentage of irrigated land to total area for the selected villages is 24 per cent and standard deviation is also 24. One-quarter of the standard deviation has been used to make a range of 18 per cent to 30 per cent for the villages with average irrigated land; while villages with irrigation more than 30 per cent have been considered in the high group and those with less than 18 per cent are in the low group. Bechraji

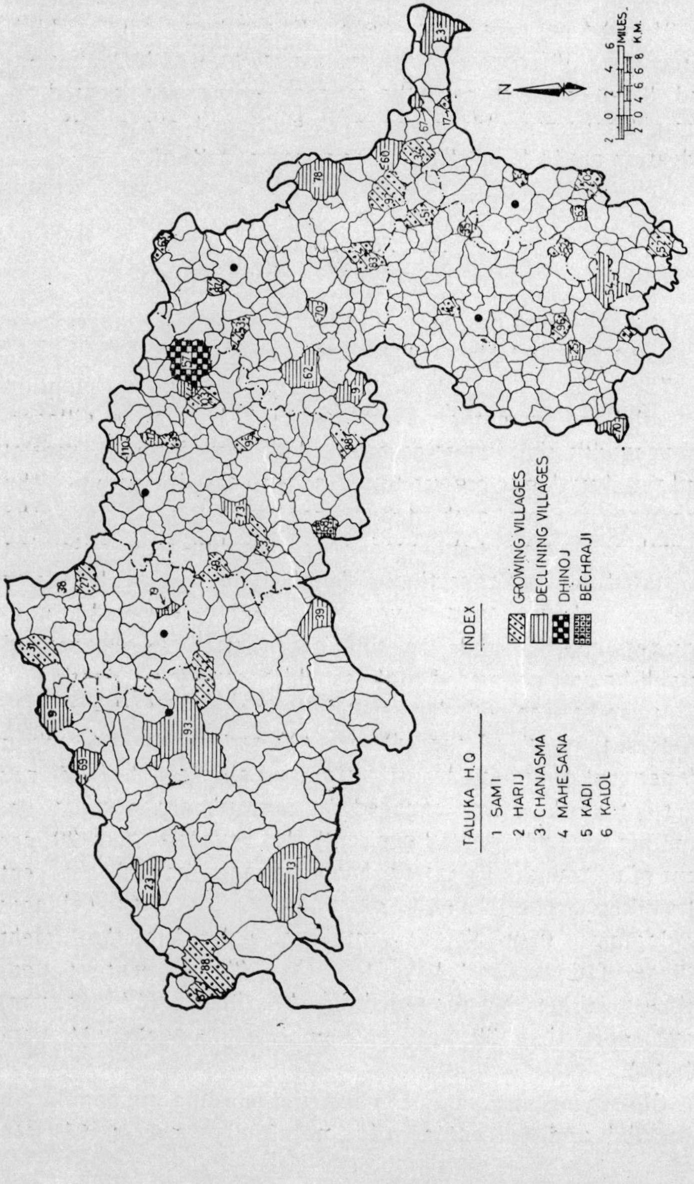

MAP 7.1: *Location of selected villages*

and Dhinoj have been omitted from this classification as these two are sampled as special cases. In this classification, the high group has 15 sample villages, average group has 14 while the low group has 22 villages in all. The mean percentages of irrigated land for the high, average and low groups are 53, 25 and 5 per cent respectively. The villages with a high percentage of irrigated land are mainly located in Mahesana and Kalol, while those in the average group are located in Harij, Chanasma, Mahesana and Kadi and those with low irrigation are in Sami, Harij, Chanasma and Kadi.

DEMOGRAPHIC AND DEVELOPMENT ASPECTS OF SELECTED VILLAGES (1981)

Demographic and development aspects of sample villages have been analysed in terms of the above classification.

There is a positive relationship between population potential and percentage of irrigated land in sample villages. Villages with high irrigation have a high population potential and the situation is reverse for those with low irrigation. The situation is same with density of population though the growth rate does not show much relationship with irrigation as stated in earlier sections. Similarly, villages with high or average irrigated land have more workers engaged in non-primary activities and are with more amenities, shops and establishments compared to those which have low irrigation.

It can be seen with further detailed analysis of the sample villages that 15 of the villages (29 per cent) have less than 20 per cent of area under irrigation and also less than 20 per cent of workers are engaged in non-primary occupations. Another nine villages (18 per cent) also have less than 20 per cent of area under irrigation, but have more than 20 per cent of workers engaged in non-primary occupations. Of the villages having more than 20 per cent area under irrigation, eight villages (16 per cent) have less than 20 per cent of non-primary workers but the remaining 19 villages (37 per cent) have more than 20 per cent non-primary workers (Appendix IV).

Classifying the sample villages according to population potential and percentage of non-primary workers, it is seen that 14 villages (27 per cent) have a population potential of less than 35,000 and up to 20 per cent non-primary workers. Another five villages (10 per cent) which also have a population potential of less than 35,000, however, have more than 20 per cent of non-primary workers. Ten villages (20 per cent) with a population potential of more than 35,000 also have less than 20 per cent non-primary workers and the remaining 22 villages (43 per cent) which have a population potential of more than 35,000 had more than 20 per cent non-primary workers and more than 20 per cent area under irrigation.

This analysis suggests that availability of irrigation, along with locational advantages, can bring about some increase in employment in the non-primary sector of economy. The conclusion has some limitations because of purposive selection of sample on the basis of growth rate in three decades: 1951-61, 1961-71, and 1971-81. For a clearer understanding of the impact of irrigation on the growth, size and economy of settlements, the sampling design should take account of growth of irrigation along with growth of population.

Selected villages have been depicted in the Triangular Graph of occupational pattern (Fig. 7.1). The triangular coordinate graph is showing the location of settlements, indicating the percentage of primary, secondary and tertiary workers. The co-ordinates are measured along lines, slanting to the right of the base, at an angle of 60°. This ensures that the three percentages of occupational types will add up to 100. The majority of selected villages have 75 to 85 per cent as primary occupation; 5 to 10 per cent as secondary occupation and 5 to 15 per cent as tertiary occupation. If a taluka as a whole is considered, Sami taluka has the highest percentage (88 per cent) of primary workers to total workers (Table 5.2), while it is lowest in Kalol taluka (57 per cent). Correlation analysis of non-primary workers of the selected villages (1971) is low with growth rate (1961-1971); "r" being .34, while the correlation is higher with density of population in 1971, "r" being .51.

The existence of shops and establishments does reflect the economic prosperity of villages with large size and high density. However, if villages are very close to large centres, shops are often not available in spite of their good economic

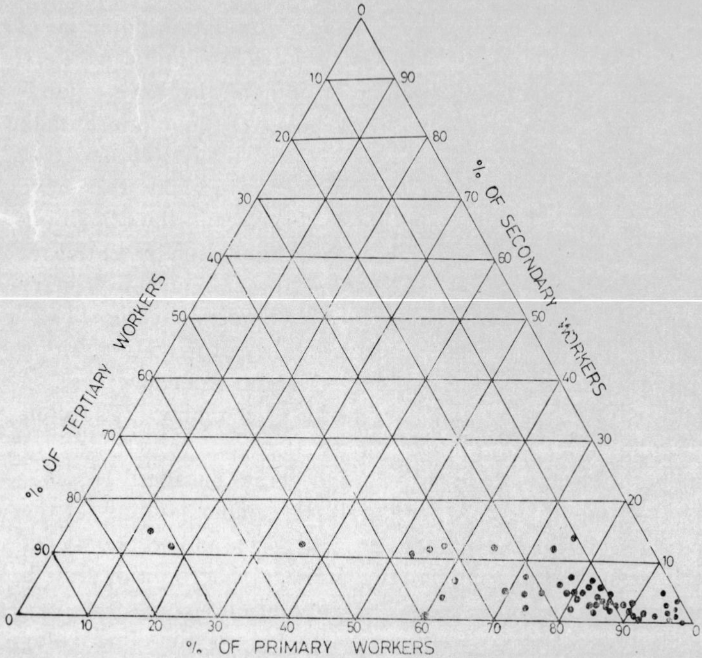

FIG. 7.1: *Triangular graph of occupation pattern for selected villages (1971)*

condition. This is due to their proximity of location to urban centres where a large number of shops are available. As a result, prosperous villages may not be serving centres for other villages.

Villagers having low purchasing power do not generally go out for shopping everyday. They tend to combine many purposes in one trip, e.g. shopping, entertainment and social visits, so that transportation cost can be minimized. As a result, sometimes a town has more attraction for villagers even if it is far away. In the western side, Sami, being a village, though a taluka headquarters, villagers prefer to go to Harij, bypassing Sami for shopping. The villages located in the northern side of Sami have economic connections outside the taluka in Radhanpur and Patan. The marketing zone of Chanasma gets shadowed by Mahesana in the east, Patan and Unjha in the north and Harij in the west. Moreover, Chanasma has to face internal competition of local markets of Bechraji in the south, Dhinoj in the north-east. Jillia and Adiwara are also two other villages providing shopping facilities in the taluka. Kadi, like Chanasma, gets sandwitched between the strong marketing influence of Mahesana in the north, Kalol in the east and Viramgam in the south-west.

Among the sample villages, the mean score for amenities, shops per 1,000 population and overall development potential is higher for villages with high irrigation than that of unirrigated villages (Appendix IV). Here again, growth rates have indicated no relationship with these variables (Table 7.1). But the total population and density of population has relationship with amenities, connectivity, frequency of bus services (Table 7.1).

TABLE 7.1 : **Correlation analysis : Demography versus connectivity, irrigation and amenities (1971)**

(*of selected 53 villages*)

X-Axis	Y-Axis	'*r*'
Total population (1971)	Weighted connectivity (1971)	.47
Density (1971)	—do—	.48
Total population (1971)	Weighted amenities (1971)	.81
Density (1971)	—do—	.35
Total population (1981)	Frequency of buses	.50
Density (1981)	—do—	.44
Growth rate (1971-81)	Connectivity (1971)	.011
Growth rate (1971-81)	Density (1981)	.009
Growth rate (1971-81)	Per cent irrigated area (1981)	-.10
Density (1981)	—do—	.56
Growth rate (1971-1981)	Development potential (1971-81)	.05
Development potential (1971-81)	Per cent irrigated area (1981)	.39

N.B. : (a) Connectivity includes metalled and unmetalled roads, fair season and all-year bus services.
(b) Amenities have been taken from the Census (30 variables).
(c) Density is persons per square km.

AN EXPERIENCE IN FIELD WORK

An experience in field work is very helpful in understanding the growth and development of villages. A distinct change is noticeable in villages if one visits them from east to west in the study area.

Mahesana and Kalol area

Villages in this side, Ambaliasan, Aldesen, Jaspur, are growing both in population and economic activities. These villages have 30 to 40 per cent of irrigated land to total land in which they harvest two or three crops a year. Cash crops and fodder crops on irrigated lands have given an extra income to villagers in the form of trade and dairy activities. Moreover, villagers are engaged in other non-primary activities in industries and services in Mahesana, Kalol, Gandhinagar and Ahmedabad. Villagers can conveniently commute to these places as the location and connectivity are very favourable.

Of these villages, Ambaliasan has developed quite well in trade and commerce based on its marketing sub-yard. Industries like tin, tiles, sawmill and paper have developed near the railway station, due to the facility of connectivity. The old cluster of the village is centred around cultivation while the new one near the railway station is based on non-primary activities and is economically prosperous.

The life-style of these villages which have connections with Ahmedabad has changed for the better with more material goods and commodities. Villagers depend on Ahmedabad for jobs, higher education and better medical facilities.

CHANASMA AREA : CASE OF DHINOJ AND BECHRAJI

Dhinoj, in the north, and Bechraji, in the south, are two important villages in Chanasma taluka. It is interesting to note that in the 1981 Census, Dhinoj has been changed from "rural" to "urban", while Bechraji has been upgraded from "rural" to "urban". According to the Census a village can be termed urban if it has a minimum population of 5,000, a density of 400 persons per square km and if 75 per cent of the male working population is engaged in non-primary occupations. It is worth looking into the historical background of these two settlements for the reasons of their change in status.

Dhinoj is an old settlement with a temple 700 years old. It is well organized with banks, hospital, public park, co-operatives and many institutions. Brahmins and the business communities (modis) live in the central part of Dhinoj, near the market, while the Harijan and Muslim communities live on the outskirts. Dhinoj used to have a thriving trade in "ghee" (butter), "gur" (molasses), brass, metal and cloth printing. With a decline in trade and commerce over a period of time, businessmen have migrated out of Dhinoj, e.g. Muslim Voras have moved to the Gulf countries, while brass makers have moved to Visanagar. A small number of Bhavsar community still exists to continue the occupation of cloth printing. With the decline of trading activities, Dhinoj could not maintain its status of township. Residents of Dhinoj talk about their glorious past as they are conscious about their economic decline.

Bechraji, in contrast to Dhinoj, has now become a focal centre. It has been a religious centre. On every full-moon day, thousands of people gather from various places for religious purposes. Taking advantage of this situation, a large number of religious, grocery and provision shops, eating places, hotels and "dharamshalas" have thrived to cater to the need of visitors. Bechraji has good connectivity and nearly 30 buses ply every day so that people can come from various places. Taking the advantage of the existing connectivity, merchants have made Bechraji an agricultural market (subyard) for collection and distribution of crops, e.g. cotton, mustard, castor, millets, etc. With an increasing non-primary activity and growing population, Bechraji earned its new status as a "town" in the 1981 Census.

In short, Dhinoj has lost its urban position due to the decline of trade, commerce and non-primary activities while Bechraji has thrived with trade and commerce along with religious functions. In Sami area, the Jain temple at Shankheshwar and the Sun temple at Modhera in Chanasma are also noted as religious centres. But none of these villages has achieved the economic status of Bechraji, as these villages have not developed much trade and commerce. Bechraji has combined both the factors of religion and trade for its development.

SAMI-HARIJ AREA

Lack of water, connectivity and low percentage of non-primary activities are the main problems of the small, scattered villages of Sami-Harij area. Water is much needed in this area both for drinking and for irrigation purposes. Villagers are engaged in harvesting one crop with the help of monsoon rains and the rest of the year many of them remain without any work. There is some seasonal migration of agricultural labour to the irrigated areas. Villages like Khakal, Rawad, Sami, Ved have grown in population but not in economic activities. The area, in general, is low in female literacy, work-participation and achievement in family planning activities. Though the economic condition is bad, the growth rate of population is high which may be related to cultural factors. These villages lack in infrastructural facilities too. Schools exist in name—neither there is a regular, qualified teacher nor are there regular students. Medical services are poor. Shops have few things to offer as villagers have low purchasing power.

To conclude, villages appear prosperous economically in the eastern side (Mahesana and Kalol) with large settlements and a higher density of population. These villages have good rainfall and soil fertility, good location and connectivity. They have a higher crop intensity with irrigation facility, higher trade and industrial activities compared to those in the western side in Sami area. No doubt all these observations have been analysed with the help of secondary data, but one gets an insight into the behavioural aspect of villagers only through field work. In many cases, villagers have no work, and they do not have any idea about the type of work that they can do. An educated, organized team is needed to give them guidance in terms of employment. Once the path is shown, the urge for work will follow.

8

CONCLUSIONS AND REFLECTIONS

MAJOR FINDINGS

(1) IN THE study area, the pattern of settlements changes gradually from the west (Sami-Harij talukas) to the east (Mahesana-Kalol talukas) in the following manner :

(a) The western side, with low irrigation and cropping intensity, has smaller settlements, widely spaced, with low density, low population potential, low connectivity, poor relative location and low level of infrastructural facilities. There is low rainfall and higher soil salinity on this side,

(b) The eastern side, with a higher level of irrigation and cropping intensity, has larger settlements, closley spaced, with high density, high population potential, high connectivity and good relative location and higher level of infrastructural facilities. Rainfall and soil fertility are higher on this side.

(2) Examining the distribution of settlements by size and density, it appears that in Kalol taluka with good irrigation, settlements have grown in size and to higher density over time (1951 to 1981). In Sami, with practically no irrigation, there has been no change of this type. It can also be noted that the correlation between the density of total population with irrigation is significantly high.

(3) Sample villages with a higher percentage of irrigated land have shown similar trends of higher density, higher population

potential, higher percentage of non-primary workers, more shops and infrastructural facilities. These villages are generally located in the eastern side, namely Mahesana and Kalol talukas. The situation is reverse for sample villages with low irrigation and are mainly located on the western side.

(4) Along with the size, distribution and density, the pattern is same from point of view of population composition—low female, literacy and low percentage of female workers in the west, while it is higher in the eastern side.

(5) In classifying settlements in terms of functional amenities of 30 types and by the size of population, it is found that the relationship is fairly high, correlation being .70. In other words, there is consistence in the system of hierarchy of larger size of population and larger number of functions in settlements. As settlements get smaller in size in the western side, so do the functions. The situation is reverse in the eastern side.

POLICY IMPLICATIONS

It is obvious from the study that there is a regional disparity in the study area in terms of "development potential". This is bound to happen as resources are not evenly distributed. To what extent the regional convergence is to be monitored depends on the value and policy of society. The government has taken up the challenge of rural development programme when the "trickling down" effect of growth centres has failed to operate in their surrounding rural areas. In order to monitor the development, many villages were provided with basic infrastructural facilities during the seventies, leading to the idea of "Place-Prosperity". This can be considered as the first step, in horizontal dimension, to remove regional disparity in short-term. This leads to the implication of a long-term policy which aims at "People-Prosperity" where the distribution is of vertical nature between groups of people within and between regions so that the general standard of living can be raised for all. In other words, amenities and facilities should be such that benefits can be reaped by the majority in society and thus the quality of human life can be improved and normalized over space.

A number of action programmes need to be implemented in

a comprehensive manner to achieve the above goal. At the outset, the rural economy needs to be vitalized. Villagers, not having irrigational facilities, have to remain idle for most of the year due to the uncertainty, variability and deficient amount of rainfall. The introduction of irrigation is essential to increase the output of land. Secondly, economy needs to be diversified with dairy and poultry farming, light industries, trade with cash crops to increase the purchasing power of villagers. Thirdly, it is essential to have a well-managed marketing agency for agrarian products so that farmers can get the best price for their produce. Fourthly, the leakage in the development programmes on infrastructural facilities neeeds to be checked. For example, primary schools may suffer from the problem of absenteeism or lack of good teachers and relevant courses for the children of farmers; or existing health centres may not be equipped well with laboratory instruments and good doctors. Subsidised, newly set industries in depressed areas may not be hiring local residents due to lack of training. It may happen that depressed regions remain areas for the supply of raw materials and do not get the chance to develop themselves. Finally, an urge to develop should come from within. Awareness and participation of villagers in development programmes are essential elements of long-term progress by which the whole community will be benefited, and the overall standard of living for the majority can be raised.

SCOPE FOR FUTURE STUDY

There is enormous scope in the study of human settlements. This study has focused only on a few aspects in a limited fashion. Planning will be relevant if our research is oriented to find out the processes of human adjustment to an evironment. Knowledge of linkage between processes and structure in a settlement-pattern can help us manipulate and plan the spatial organization that we desire to have by monitoring the mobilization of resources. Detailed data are necessary, at village level, on migration in order to know the process that controls the structure. Similarly, detailed economic data are necessary to understand the growth and decline of rural economy so that development planning can be monitored.

APPENDICES

APPENDIX 1

POPULATION OF VILLAGES

SAMI TALUKA

Sl. No.	Name of village	Population			
		1951	1961	1971	1981 (estimated)
1.	Adgam	359	480	676	730
2.	Anvarpura	314	560	684	1176
3.	Aritha	491	667	843	1239
4.	Islampura	143	127	250	397
5.	Upaliyasara	264	367	550	737
6.	Umedpur	181	251	421	475
7.	Orumana	298	757	1039	1475
8.	Kathiwada	198	291	299	472
9.	Kanij	529	819	1077	1475
10.	Kathi	358	489	702	996
11.	Kukmana	1394	1663	2125	2890
12.	Kuvarad	903	1137	1655	2134
*13.	Kuvar	981	1433	2151	2710
14.	Kokta	173	437	417	467
15.	Kodadha	195	264	379	401
16.	Kanchanpura	196	205	401	565
17.	Karchariya	216	474	608	614
18.	Khijadiyali	426	435	709	1063
19.	Khandiya	100	118	204	349
20.	Gajdinpura	458	660	1003	1384
21.	Gujarwada	473	686	1057	1278
22.	Gochnad	1316	1599	2173	2694
*23.	Godhana	571	660	801	1009
24.	Chandardi	194	295	475	579
25.	Jalalabad	240	246	380	471
26.	Jahurpura	86	142	224	211
27.	Jakhel	292	298	529	749
28.	Jesda	341	367	544	778
29.	Zilwana	765	930	1261	1475
30.	Tuvad	1079	1453	1948	2649
31.	Taranagar	242	446	762	1166

*Selected villages

1	2	3	4	5
32. Tarora	441	609	787	999
33. Dandpur	283	401	558	680
34. Dadka	308	352	447	543
35. Dadar	298	742	1007	1349
36. Dantisana	471	584	780	959
37. Dudkha	1305	1796	2674	3583
38. Dhadhana	943	1240	1496	1959
*39. Dhanora	452	691	1075	1354
40. Nana Joranarpura	207	280	407	537
41. Nani Chandur	1024	1425	1809	2550
42. Nayaka	629	1106	1506	1897
43. Padla	1272	1583	2284	2969
44. Palipur	178	214	347	507
45. Pirojpura	260	418	569	739
46. Panchasar	1505	1973	2676	3291
47. Fatehganj	204	292	415	602
48. Fatehpura	139	231	350	476
49. Badargani	117	153	192	309
50. Babri	242	1374	565	717
51. Baspa	890	1269	1582	2341
52. Bilia	392	526	719	292
53. Bismillabad	139	117	204	295
54. Buda	390	519	702	947
55. Bobra	506	568	950	1244
56. Bhadrada	488	961	1558	1994
57. Bhamathal	191	366	480	585
58. Mardanganj	71	102	196	288
59. Mohammadpura	353	511	873	934
60. Matrota	529	612	816	1004
61. Mandvi	906	1242	1662	2127
62. Munjpur	1985	2941	2957	3755
63. Murtuzanagar	49	48	68	72
64. Mubarakpura	269	342	514	648
65. Mamna	440	616	799	1071
66. Mota-Joravapura	449	589	839	1048
67. Moti-Chandur	1401	1797	2207	2913
68. Mankodia	53	90	146	175
*69. Ranawada	556	800	1148	1423
70. Ranod	663	490	956	1262
71. Rakanpura	226	293	460	566
*72. Ravad	657	703	965	1303
73. Rasulpura	242	300	387	538

*Selected villages

(*Contd.*)

1	2	3	4	5
74. Rajpura	214	346	537	661
75. Rafoo	825	1312	2057	2468
76. Rampura	315	457	675	824
77. Runi	177	169	452	579
78. Rupnagar	263	364	597	794
79. Lalpur	162	210	567	811
80. Loteshwar	248	309	488	547
81. Loida	1477	1942	2758	3723
82. Varana	699	959	1373	1840
83. Vagosana	396	501	775	1023
84. Vaghapura	229	353	562	680
85. Vaghel	1017	1470	1971	2484
86. Vaval	202	353	434	590
*87. Vahedpura	275	463	663	988
*88. Ved	966	1286	1774	2750
89. Samsherpura	266	556	834	1126
90. Sherpura	333	553	770	932
91. Shankheshwar	1419	1681	2773	3965
92. Sajupura	227	239	353	469
*93. Sami	5422	6613	7416	9641
94. Sipur	641	870	1149	1586
95. Sukhpura	87	158	306	459
96. Subapura	333	426	635	851
97. Sonar	285	383	529	667

*Selected villages

HARIJ TALUKA

Sl. No.	Name of village	Population 1951	1961	1971	1981
1.	Adia	1738	2270	2594	3044
2.	Eklra	1026	1104	1476	1867
3.	Kalana	443	548	752	893
4.	Kathi	893	1132	1611	2056
5.	Katra	1050	1267	1791	2134
6.	Kurija	580	826	976	1272
7.	Kumbhana	461	576	760	961
8.	Khekhdi	500	691	863	1035
*9.	Khakhal	563	988	1322	1388
10.	Govna	516	762	961	1205
11.	Chabkha	330	356	450	515
12.	Jannanapura	911	1241	1657	2024
13.	Jashvantpura	336	502	452	592
14.	Jasornav	464	611	822	1011
15.	Jaoka	449	547	707	954
16.	Toranipura	88	137	200	245
17.	Tanibolia	734	981	1207	1439
18.	Tharod	301	430	562	841
*19.	Dantarwada	373	574	798	902
20.	Dunawada	1391	1849	2339	2755
21.	Nana	676	865	1099	1485
22.	Palai	127	189	237	373
23.	Piplana	1288	1845	1981	2311
24.	Piluwada	175	248	363	448
25.	Baratwada	1255	1579	1886	2517
26.	Bhalavia	289	402	505	560
*27.	Malsund	458	530	583	804
28.	Masa	301	501	649	688
29.	Manka Nava + Juna	1305	1781	2355	3123
30.	Ravindra	739	1033	1152	1469
*31.	Roda	1475	1801	2219	3018
32.	Raghunathpura	499	588	729	853
33.	Vansa	1129	1603	1923	2074
34.	Vejawada	474	735	1104	1294
35.	Sarval	175	764	1212	1394
36.	Savel	514	685	900	1093
37.	Sarasada				45
*38.	Sankara	297	1596	1893	2080
39.	Sodhav	769	937	1098	1441
40.	Harij Town	6963	8965	11073	14837

* Selected villages

CHANASMA TALUKA

Sl. No.	Name of village	Population			
		1951	1961	1971	1981
1.	Ajabpura	149	213	248	288
2.	Aakba	630	799	1076	1248
*3.	Adiwada	1032	1238	1474	1803
4.	Asijol	1076	1321	1671	2034
5.	Itoda	890	1256	1574	1901
6.	Indrap	239	265	398	561
7.	Ishlampura	751	976	1194	1381
8.	Udela	272	335	448	468
9.	Endala	530	709	925	1212
10.	Ambala	1249	1588	1864	2245
11.	Kakasana	211	204	161	271
12.	Kancda	1250	1462	1722	1960
13.	Kumalpur	322	425	561	621
14.	Karan Sagar	259	424	610	851
15.	Karoda	492	611	800	997
16.	Kalri	2249	2736	3172	4072
*17.	Kesni	810	1087	1330	1464
18.	Kambai	2850	3278	3823	4254
19.	Kharadharva	530	687	873	964
20.	Kharidhariyal	1117	1523	1903	2229
21.	Khambhal	1213	1523	1798	2320
22.	Khokhla	285	330	392	470
23.	Kharasan	1070	1292	1612	1927
24.	Galolivasna	301	447	467	666
25.	Gambhu	1989	2722	3226	3940
26.	Gobharva	620	807	847	938
27.	Garad	1681	2107	2616	2914
28.	Ganget	867	1170	1391	1589
29.	Chadasana	1040	1421	1203	1424
30.	Chevell	1528	1823	2174	2972
31.	Chandanki	369	457	544	489
32.	Chandrada	480	698	868	1126
33.	Chhatasana	293	384	467	606
34.	Chhaniadiher	1139	1382	1913	2069
35.	Jasalpur	621	920	1180	1670
36.	Jakhana	1053	1248	1347	1473
37.	Jitoda	1091	1419	1642	1714
38.	Jetpur	1200	1505	1796	2232
*39.	Jilla	324	458	798	1419

* Selected villages

1	2	3	4	5
40. Jilliavasana	82	421	509	555
41. Takodi	824	1210	1758	2045
42. Dedana	1240	1585	1833	2130
43. Dadivada	967	1291	1670	2093
*44. Dandoarda	967	898	1020	1147
45. Dantkarodi	556	683	874	939
46. Dethil	785	926	1240	1372
47. Dedarda	190	269	324	450
48. Delparakant	599	515	608	750
*49. Dehual	1277	1570	1948	2705
50. Dedwadokhant	825	866	1187	1466
51. Devghar			592	779
52. Dhanpura	320	330	624	818
53. Dharmoda	774	1035	1270	1833
54. Dhanodharda	967	1282	1536	1833
55. Dharpuri	291	367	428	531
56. Dharpuri Khant	599	705	929	1380
*57. Dhinoj	6423	7580	8964	10540
58. Nalanpura	139	173	191	141
59. Palasar	1963	2129	2650	3042
60. Pindharpura	965	1178	1515	1618
61. Pimpal	1439	1725	1887	2205
62. Poyda	307	314	380	554
63. Panchasal	398	420	728	859
64. Platapghar	399	542	648	744
65. Fitchaddi	739	935	1244	1661
66. Fichal	659	791	905	1155
67. Bariet	529	625	903	771
*68. Bechraji	1743	2645	4452	8904
69. Blahmanwada	1828	2097	2535	2953
70. Bhagamada	632	668	902	987
71. Bhalvasana	467	583	714	932
72. Bhatsar	1080	1449	1699	1901
*73. Maniyari	1495	1840	2127	2149
74. Matlasam	304	443	476	671
75. Mithidharva	1006	1312	1461	1457
76. Mithi Dhariyal	1399	1657	2052	2674
77. Muthania	228	304	388	661
78. Merwada	1039	1334	1603	1609
79. Mesra	77	166	113	216
80. Motap	1760	2067	2334	2773
81. Modhera	2398	3162	4198	5000

* Selected villages

(*Contd.*)

1	2	3	4	5
82. Mandlop	514	839	900	1160
83, Mandali	546	631	780	1110
84. Ranchhopura	383	460	530	489
85. Ranasan	738	1018	1183	1405
86. Ranela	820	1004	1335	1580
87. Rampura	424	560	732	1041
*88. Rantej	1255	1765	2368	3048
89. Ruppura	945	1228	1405	1813
90. Ruppura	995	831	1418	1772
91. Lanva Karanpura	1787	2107	2493	2810
92. Vadavali	3085	3825	4823	5328
93. Vanpura	67	52	113	993
94. Vasai	1499	1811	2368	2456
*95. Vijapurda	604	871	1213	1467
96. Virta	1313	1449	1774	2071
97. Venpura	628	773	839	135
98. Saduthala	625	749	963	1194
99. Sardarpura	337	390	519	656
100. Sarsav	592	705	929	965
101. Sanpawada	1072	1400	1862	2298
102. Suganpura	345	467	527	638
*103. Sanasar	2454	2764	3560	4579
104. Surpura	753	996	1325	1378
105. Surag	401	616	910	1279
106. Selavi	632	6675	819	735
107. Sevala	930	1348	1616	1873
108. Sendhal	714	989	1266	1530
109. Sedha	627	840	1018	1354
*110. Sojitra	662	869	1076	1096
111. Sankhalpur	2492	3128	3575	4213
112. Chanasma Town	11035	12106	14398	16125

*Selected villages

MAHESANA TALUKA

Sl. No.	Name of village	Population			
		1951	1961	1971	1981
1.	Ajabpura	499	620	833	955
2.	Aloda	881	1104	1327	1644
3.	Adkhaj	1852	2500	3181	3862
*4.	Ambaliasan	1274	1716	3001	3901
5.	Ijpura-Jethaji	446	574	737	790
6.	Ijpura-Barot	398	541	625	712
7.	Uiharpi	501	583	701	785
8.	Amnasan	2523	2869	3464	4058
9.	Kolosan	2119	2641	3282	3401
10.	Kadvasan	559	655	978	1160
11.	Kasanpura	293	409	550	682
12.	Kasalpura	643	862	1062	1207
13.	Kanpura	273	398	553	702
14.	Kukar	850	1180	1407	1957
15.	Kochra	425	458	651	776
16.	Khadalpur	988	1156	1322	1652
17.	Khara	1114	1330	1808	2281
18.	Kherva	3753	4421	5554	5708
19.	Gamanpura	630	917	1107	1218
20.	Gilasan	232	310	474	521
21.	Beratpur	121	149	242	222
22.	Gokalpura	333	416	528	602
23.	Ghadha	1011	1070	1317	1672
24.	Charadu	2308	2683	3174	3491
25.	Chalura	1528	1848	2306	2770
26.	Chitrodipura	376	561	697	919
27.	Chhathiarda	2200	2633	3212	3759
28.	Jagudan	2383	2905	3608	5078
29.	Jamanpur	510	534	734	850
30.	Kakasana	1177	1329	1806	1932
31.	Junisedhavi	571	644	814	935
32.	Jetalpur	514	685	845	986
33.	Jotana	3424	4661	5666	6739
34.	Jornang	2319	2813	3666	4546
35.	Tundali	797	912	1354	1575
36.	Tareti	703	887	1047	1820
37.	Tawadia	578	764	935	706
38.	Tejpura	565	695	853	830
39.	Ditasana	270	346	403	556

*Selected villages

(*Contd.*)

1	2	3	4	5
40. Divanpura	704	868	1111	1185
41. Dediasan	1079	1491	1975	2338
42. Dela	789	950	1111	1454
43. Delol	907	1210	1443	1804
44. Devrasan	1374	1701	2100	2238
45. Devinapura	594	752	990	1082
46. Dhanpura	371	350	602	764
47. Dhandhasan	802	989	1186	1344
48. Dholasan	1354	1700	2078	2366
49. Nadasa	1251	1661	2095	2405
50. Navi Sedhavi	603	676	876	1104
51. Nagalper	0001	1414	1897	3443
52. Manidan	1087	1409	1897	3443
*53. Naugar	1354	1630	2007	2712
54. Chalua	1101	1304	1559	2343
55. Palaj	918	1104	1513	1798
56. Palrasana	858	1103	1361	2356
57. Paloda	1829	2190	2860	3424
58. Panchat	3614	4584	5917	7029
59. Pilodra	2019	2619	3309	3869
60. Punasan	913	1132	1388	1518
61. Balvanlpura	217	272	308	421
*62. Balol	3058	3739	4484	5141
*63. Bamuoana	1665	1927	2254	3178
64. Baliasana	793	907	1195	1388
65. Buttg Paldi	1048	1271	1545	1795
66. Bcdla	522	637	759	1374
67. Bariavi	2225	2667	3427	4245
68. Bhakadia	318	500	617	648
69. Bhasaria	1018	1148	1506	1695
*70. Bhesana	963	1282	1680	1865
71. Magona	1844	2255	2663	3333
72. Natriku	810	926	1297	1440
73. Mareda	901	1195	1572	1897
74. Manknay	2041	2536	3079	3457
75. Mitha	777	984	1351	1468
76. Mudanda	1438	1776	2406	2675
77. Mulsan	1072	1308	1685	2029
*78. Meu	3319	4269	4937	6024
79. Mohmuedpura	894	995	1211	1415
80. Mewad	965	1151	1571	1814
81. Motidan	2131	2630	3342	3898
82. Modipura	567	655	833	951

*Selected villages

1	2	3	4	5
*83. Mandali	748	913	1368	1601
84. Ranipura	397	481	600	714
85. Rampura-L	358	448	611	714
86. Rampura-K	822	1013	1290	1544
*87. Ramosana	465	619	880	1179
88. Rupal	308	368	428	414
89. Lakhwad	1693	2291	2953	3493
90. Laghnaj	5205	6110	6826	8364
91. Linch	4546	5268	6403	7742
*92. Vadasama	2822	3262	4246	5018
93. Vadasan	1204	1503	1899	2215
94. Virsoda	1036	1233	1501	1669
95. Sakhapurda	253	336	441	514
96. Sametra	1353	1611	2128	2440
97. Sakdi	1607	1878	2673	3020
98. Sanghapur	1170	1340	1628	1993
99. Santhal	2047	2190	2935	3434
100. Sidosan	419	502	578	517
101. Sobhasan	849	1047	1338	1604
102. Hardesan	318	421	512	629
103. Harsandal	548	768	975	1058
104. Haripura	197	263	391	454
105. Hadvi	312	394	531	616
106. Higlajanpura	376	502	663	883
107. Heduva Rajgar	362	540	658	825
108. Hedura Hanumant	280	374	655	714
109. Behura	437	582	771	996
110. Mahesana Town	22804	32577	51713	72915

*Selected villages

KADI TALUKA

Sl. No.	Name of village	Population 1951	1961	1971	1981
1.	Agal	1981	2329	2796	3102
2.	Acharasan	478	645	830	1001
3.	Ankhal	438	492	617	767
*4.	Aldesan	971	1142	1349	1672
5.	Adaraj	2308	2691	3638	4212
6.	Aduara	1361	1496	1982	2333
7.	Anandpura	488	579	743	854
8.	Alampur	256	350	524	566
9.	Alusana	152	175	226	320
10.	Ambaliara	365	527	673	756
11.	Indrad	1365	1557	2165	2665
12.	Irana	1000	1092	1582	1791
13.	Ishwarpura	88	100	112	120
14.	Uniwa	1065	1114	1530	1818
15.	Ambavpura	421	501	644	761
16.	Kujari	508	715	803	1000
17.	Karijisan	1715	2227	2506	2932
18.	Karan Nagar	2174	2649	3348	3921
19.	Karran Pura	469	563	879	1045
20.	Kalyanpura	1708	2600	2884	3143
21.	Kasana	1301	1556	1996	2435
22.	Kundal	1326	1609	2058	3111
23.	Kaiyal	1564	1482	2219	2684
*24.	Kalad	960	1012	1167	1596
25.	Karada	931	1165	1350	1606
26.	Knaved	1779	2211	2582	2840
27.	Kherpur	520	584	881	929
28.	Khandmova	114	115	163	228
*29.	Khanderapura	496	728	1042	1272
30.	Ganeshpura	482	590	807	1160
31.	Goladra	356	464	564	682
32.	Govindpura	344	490	571	708
33.	Ghugala	225	304	370	502
34.	Ghumasan	1833	2342	2991	3619
*35.	Chadasana	681	828	1080	1188
36.	Charoi	1110	1340	1547	1976
37.	Chalasan	772	812	1032	1172
38.	Chandrad	481	558	690	
39.	Chandrasan	757	1080	1364	1495
40.	Chhalesara	403	519	604	774

*Selected villages

1	2	3	4	5
41. Jamiyatpura	289	252	274	395
42. Jadupura	210	207	297	351
43. Jaralpur	1411	1664	2042	2133
44. Jetoura	349	380	501	558
45. Jerangpura	581	726	838	952
46. Jhaloda	873	1062	1374	1695
47. Jhulasan	2249	2695	3717	4720
48. Jankhiya	369	419	530	684
49. Daran	2315	2711	3168	3833
50. Daranmorva	283	321	414	508
*51. Dangarva	3488	3958	4807	5915
52. Dhoria	580	693	886	1071
53. Jhadod	418	474	709	708
*54. Thol	2589	3525	4376	4843
55. Digadi	372	457	630	707
56. Dhudhai	178	231	251	374
57. Devsana	819	1071	1471	1685
58. Della	334	414	522	633
59. Dhanali	821	1007	1329	1630
60. Drandhalpur	194	235	280	334
61. Dhalasan	386	456	666	746
62. Nagrasan	703	796	1050	1223
63. Nadan	431	563	751	891
64. Narsipura	610	737	919	1140
65. Nadolia	212	272	361	398
66. Nanpura Wadasan	344	404	491	561
67. Nanikadi	905	1194	1424	1965
68. Narola	1054	1173	1534	1890
69. Nandasan	3510	4034	5542	5826
*70. Palli	751	819	946	1003
71. Pirojpur	360	504	588	735
72. Panthoda	677	895	1059	1143
73. Fatehpura	129	161	191	228
74. Fuletea	1204	1537	1856	2184
75. Balasar	1065	1359	1522	1675
76. Babajipura	309	344	366	506
77. Bavla	1507	1792	2284	2584
78. Budasan	308	341	552	679
79. Barisana	977	1087	1435	1843
80. Bhatsan	1043	1145	1362	1557
81. Bhalthi	1381	1671	1937	2303
82. Manipur	683	785	910	1189
83. Maharajpura	534	573	704	852

*Selected villages

(*Contd.*)

1	2	3	4	5
84. Mathasal	1305	1469	1801	1953
85. Medha	752	928	1146	1330
86. Merda	82	92	139	162
87. Mokasan	1033	1196	1440	1520
88. Movan	247	298	386	463
89. Yasvantpura	329	512	610	685
90. Rajpur	3181	3634	4398	4734
91. Rozapuri	94	89	111	156
92. Raghupura	685	867	1079	1343
93. Laxmanpura	701	930	1162	1354
94. Laximipura	328	376	440	953
95. Lunasan	866	1113	1283	1373
*96. Lhar	688	755	900	1161
97. Vadavi	1200	1436	1719	2071
98. Vadu	2139	2683	3317	3794
99. Vansal	627	762	879	1137
100. Varkhadia	819	1044	1273	1431
101. Valavadi	71	164	264	424
102. Vadhadoda	1143	1311	1689	1697
103. Vamaj	2144	2583	3345	3910
104. Vidaj	1180	1372	1685	1920
105. Vinayakpura	365	402	457	520
106. Visadpura	981	1269	1542	1641
107. Visalpura	363	425	654	630
108. Vejra	864	1005	1277	1427
109. Shiapura	365	451	541	676
110. Sareav	1111	1287	1612	1872
111. Sadra	1035	1289	1606	1959
112. Sujatpura	353	440	605	674
113. Suraj	2284	2674	3284	3673
114. Seodra	127	154	210	209
115. Shedardi	551	654	622	909
116. Shedrana	391	500	784	721
117. Hripura	239	251	278	306
118. Kadi Town	20373	23661	28332	35415

*Selected villages

KALOL TALUKA

Sl. No.	Name of village	Population 1951	1961	1971	1981
1.	Adhana	124	176	260	297
2.	Amrapur	333	496	1014	1456
*3.	Aluva	936	1022	1318	1479
4.	Aamja	1220	1460	1901	2287
*5.	Aarsodia	490	639	965	1160
6.	Itta	573	608	810	1037
7.	Isand	1683	2199	2603	3154
8.	Unali	441	538	645	808
9.	Usmanabad	573	573	615	676
10.	Ola	654	803	1045	1232
11.	Karoli	509	592	735	865
12.	Kantha	1340	1700	2154	2472
13.	Khatraj	442	534	754	742
14.	Kharajdabhi	1625	1514	2014	2114
15.	Ganpatpura	79	77	121	155
16.	Golthara	1482	1896	2378	2905
*17.	Chandisana	807	921	1213	1540
18.	Chhatral	2409	2971	3983	4600
19.	Jawla	2217	2500	3276	3661
*20.	Jaspur	1358	1588	2020	2473
21.	Jethlaj	868	1066	1447	1754
22.	Dingocha	2192	2571	3196	3932
23.	Dantali	211	284	333	330
24.	Dhamasana	2078	2397	3192	3861
25.	Dhanaj	776	1060	1386	1823
26.	Dhanotra	282	383	619	662
27.	Dhendshu	368	463	589	822
28.	Nava	147	261	351	420
29.	Nadri	388	390	471	739
30.	Nardipur	4041	4676	5859	7290
31.	Nasmed	900	1190	1484	1747
32.	Nandoli	272	347	503	702
33.	Palsana	1163	1505	2009	2434
*34.	Paliyad	3623	3930	4893	5529
35.	Palvodia	347	458	555	658
36.	Pansar	3197	3782	5039	6426
37.	Piyaj	1352	1744	2109	2417
38.	Pratappura	447	577	790	1079
39.	Balra	2384	2719	3903	5425

*Selected villages

(*Contd.*)

1	2	3	4	5
40. Bileshwarpura	431	483	639	763
41. Baisana	1911	2371	2938	3633
42. Bhedol	485	543	745	947
43. Bhwpura	419	567	740	943
44. Bhimasana	273	377	554	681
45. Bhayanmati	2100	2430	2871	3161
46. Mubarakpura	716	789	557	569
47. Mulsana	298	372	557	569
48. Mobhasan	1427	1836	2473	3103
49. Rakanpur	543	612	759	892
50. Ranchhaslpura	417	486	560	597
51. Ramnagar	609	756	999	1263
*52. Rancherda	1389	1671	1890	2066
53. Limbodra	2753	2779	3851	4621
54. Vadsar	1850	1906	2511	3666
55. Vadavswami	504	699	980	1105
56. Vagosan	845	945	1323	1336
57. Vayna	654	860	1071	1076
*58. Vansjada K	762	1027	1427	1610
59. Vansajada Dhedia	471	552	766	925
*60. Veda	2018	2977	4005	4666
61. Saij	3958	4114	5089	8448
62. Sanavad	239	291	388	466
*63. Sabaspur	843	967	1117	1241
64. Santej	2064	2511	2877	3276
65. Serisa	2088	2529	2881	3426
66. Soja	3511	4062	5477	6756
*67. Sabhasar	572	727	1021	1220
68. Hajipur	1304	1748	1845	2398
69. Kalol Town	22432	31940	50321	69946

*Selected villages

APPENDIX II

WEIGHTED AMENITIES OF VILLAGES (1971)
(On the Basis of Scarcity Principle)

Sl. No.	Type of amenities	Weighted points
1.	Primary school	2
2.	Secondary school	87
3.	College	99
4.	Industrial School	99
5.	Training School	99
6.	Other Institutions	90
7.	Hospital	98
8.	Maternity Home	97
9.	Child Welfare Centre	99
10.	Health Centre	96
11.	Dispensary	87
12.	Family Planning Centre	94
13.	Electricity for all purposes	98
14.	Electricity for Agriculture	75
15.	Tap water	74
16.	Well	8
17.	Tube-well	80
18.	Tank	76
19.	River and others	93
20.	Pucca road	71
21.	Kutcha road	18
22.	Railway station	86
23.	Whole year bus service	76
24.	Fair season	48
25.	Post Office	67
26.	Post & Telegraph Office	98
27.	Telephone	93

APPENDIX III

TABLE (A) : Irrigated land by major crops and by taluka during 1965-68 and 1975-78

(*in hectare*)

Taluka	Sami		Harij		Chanasma		Mahesana		Kedi		Kalol	
Total area for 3 year period	1965 to 1968	1975 to 1978	1965 to 1968	1975 to 1978	1965 to 1968	1975 to 1978	1965 to 1968	1975 to 1978	1965 to 1968	1975 to 1978	1965 to 1968	1975 to 1978
(1)	(2)	(3)	(4)	(5)	(6)	(7)	(8)	(9)	(10)	(11)	(12)	(13)
Bajri	—	—	—	114	937	949	275	6730	200	4589	352	9202
Wheat	845	186	5867	6402	5929	6884	23646	21426	21389	16923	14074	18741
Condiments	—	2977	4	5207	188	—	221	6955	151	2762	300	—
Cotton	—	—	—	1300	12327	2858	16270	25082	14985	25368	17380	18140
Fodder	133	87	458	469	395	7348	2884	4870	1395	6056	1247	1358

N.B. : Mean irrigated land in the study area:
1965-1968 = 71,319 hectare
1975-1978 = 107,924 hectare

Source : Directorate of Agriculture, Govt. of Gujarat.

TABLE (B) : **Mean per cent share of major crops on irrigated land during 1965-68 and 1975-78**

Crops	Mean irrigated area in hectare		Per cent change	Per cent share of total irrigated land	
	1965-68	1975-78		1965-68	1975-78
Bajri	588	7195	+1124	.82	6.6
Wheat	23917	23521	—1.65	33.50	21.7
Condiments	288	5967	+1972	.40	5.5
Cotton	20321	24249	+ 19	28.50	22.4
Fodder	2170	6729	+ 210	3.0	6.2

N.B. : Mean total irrigated area 1965-68= 71319 hectares
Mean total irrigated area 1975-78=107924 hectares

Source : Directorate of Agriculture, Govt. of Gujarat.

APPENDIX IV

TABLE (A) : Sample Villages—with low percentage of irrigated land (<18 per cent)—(1981)

Sl. No.	Village No. (Taluka)	Village name	% of irrigated land to total land (1981)	Population (1981) total	Growth rate of population (1971-81)	Population potential (1981)	Density (hectare) '81	% of non primary workers to total workers (1981)	Amenities Score' 81	Shops per 1000 population (1981)	Development potential ('71-'81)
(1)	(2)	(3)	(4)	(5)	(6)	(7)	(8)	(9)	(10)	(11)	(12)
1.	87 (S)	Vahedpur	0.00	986	48.72	15017	1.11	1.40	75	8.00	81
2.	72 (S)	Read	2.30	1301	34.82	37259	.71	16.26	140	3.07	112
3.	88 (S)	Ved	0.00	2423	36.58	16446	.68	17.98	181	5.78	137
4.	93 (S)	Sami	0.00	9624	29.77	27625	1.53	37.32	579	10.68	352
5.	23 (S)	Godhara	0.00	1009	25.97	20372	.55	13.84	140	5.95	91
6.	13 (S)	Kunkar	0.00	2706	25.80	19646	.62	8.72	211	1.85	145
7.	39 (S)	Dhanora	0.00	1358	26.32	29879	.92	7.10	149	2.94	104
8.	69 (S)	Ranawada	0.00	1415	23.26	22083	1.40	7.27	40	1.41	78
9.	27 (H)	Malsund	4.05	804	37.91	29219	.78	7.28	68	4.98	169
10.	9 (H)	Khakhal	0.00	1384	4.69	24096	.78	17.54	60	1.44	111

11.	19 (H)	Dantarwada	10.75	902	13.03	38156	2.94	3.83	169	4.43	135
12.	39 (Ch)	Jillia	12.30	1419	77.82	40012	2.53	48.96	365	.78	207
13.	88 (Ch)	Rantej	4.63	3048	28.72	39169	1.57	23.24	208	9.60	186
14.	95 (Ch)	Vijapwada	6.67	1467	20.94	43072	2.44	21.88	173	2.73	169
15.	103 (Ch)	Sunsar	9.85	4584	28.76	43652	4.10	5.91	152	2.83	141
16.	3 (Ch)	Adiwada	12.59	1898	28.76	39034	2.39	20.67	89	3.16	176
17.	92 (M)	Vadasma	13.82	5018	18.18	52402	2.42	27.05	412	1.20	180
18.	9 (M)	Kotosan	3.71	3392	3.35	41795	2.42	25.96	261	2.65	171
19.	29 (K)	Khanderupura	12.60	1272	22.07	29641	5.17	14.84	256	10.20	172
20.	96 (K)	Lhor	6.58	1161	29.00	38602	1.41	25.71	138	6.03	120
21.	24 (K)	Kolad	9.32	1596	36.76	33290	1.16	15.74	124	3.76	128
22.	58 (Kl)	Vansjada	6.90	1610	12.82	39585	3.08	4.28	139	3.10	115
	Total (Mean)		5.59	2363	28.49	34259	1.99	17.14	194	4.53	154

APPENDIX IV—(Contd.)

TABLE (B) : **Sample villages—with high percentage of irrigated land (> 30%)**

Sl. No.	Village No. (Taluka)	Village name	per cent of irrigated land to total land 1981	Population 1981 Total	Growth rate of population (1971-81)	Population potential 1981	Density (hectare) 1981	per cent of non-primary workers to total workers 1981	Amenities score 1981	Shops per 1000 population 1981	Development potential (1971-81)
(1)	(2)	(3)	(4)	(5)	(6)	(7)	(8)	(9)	(10)	(11)	(12)
1.	49 (Ch)	Delmal	36.83	2706	38.91	37158	1.66	11.98	158	5.54	205
2.	87 (M)	Ramosan	40.82	1180	34.09	43140	3.44	58.17	170	5.90	180
3.	53 (M)	Nugar	54.55	2712	35.13	46239	3.09	39.14	259	4.80	172
4.	63 (M)	Bamosana	83.92	3183	41.21	34066	5.38	31.21	242	3.14	215
5.	83 (M)	Mandali	42.44	1601	17.03	57102	2.75	21.81	145	5.62	185
6.	70 (M)	Bhesana	65.41	1873	11.49	55328	3.36	24.71	193	3.20	192
7.	4 (K)	Aldesan	32.53	1672	23.94	46752	2.67	22.63	207	3.00	177
8.	5 (KL)	Arsodia	51.33	1160	20.21	35587	4.41	37.91	118	5.17	185
9.	17 (KL)	Chandisana	74.23	1544	27.29	35550	6.74	13.82	186	1.94	201
10.	34 (KL)	Paliad	70.14	5543	13.28	42567	3.88	29.47	412	4.33	253
11.	20 (KL)	Jaspur	34.63	2473	22.42	29064	2.74	34.09	388	7.68	183
12.	3 (KL)	Alanka	42.32	1479	12.21	24928	1.18	14.72	152	2.03	157
13.	63 (KL)	Sabaspur	32.69	1241	11.10	36400	3.43	15.52	116	8.06	109
14.	60 (KL)	Veda	42.81	4667	16.53	44200	3.57	32.80	426	1.93	233
15.	67 (KL)	Sobhasan	87.05	1220	19.49	35135	4.40	12.77	176	3.28	199
	Total (Mean)		53.41	2365	24.25	42557	3.80	27.57	235	4.59	203

TABLE (C) : **Sample villages—with average percentage of irrigated land (Mean range considered (18% to 30%)**

Sl. No.	Village No. (Taluka)	Village name	per cent of irrigated land to total land 1981	Population (1981) Total	Growth rate (1971-81)	Population potential 1981	Density (hectare) 1981	per cent of non primary workers to total workers 1981	Amenities score 1981	Shops per 1000 population 1981	Development potential (1971-81)
(1)	(2)	(3)	(4)	(5)	(6)	(7)	(8)	(9)	(10)	(11)	(12)
1.	31 (H)	Roda	18.13	3011	35.69	24489	1.54	10.06	301	5.30	146
2.	38 (H)	Sankara	26.58	2080	9.88	44541	1.68	20.36	270	7.20	123
3.	44 (CH)	Danodarda	28.79	1147	12.45	44418	2.56	9.65	119	2.61	153
4.	73 (CH)	Maniyaru	21.29	2149	1.03	47854	2.01	17.62	237	3.72	166
5.	17 (CH)	Kesri	22.27	1464	10.07	38526	3.26	35.23	211	5.46	159
6.	110 (CH)	Sojitra	23.61	1096	1.86	33995	1.41	20.99	115	2.74	196
7.	4 (M)	Ambaliyasan	27.83	3892	29.99	53058	10.03	76.34	456	19.50	364
8.	62 (M)	Balol	20.66	5040	12.40	44420	2.92	25.51	444	6.94	220
9.	78 (M)	Meu	23.62	6024	22.02	41693	2.35	24.83	337	5.64	229
10.	51 (M)	Dangarva	20.43	5925	23.26	57163	3.29	50.78	510	4.22	312
11.	70 (K)	Pali	24.97	1002	5.91	26185	1.10	5.00	134	2.00	121
12.	54 (K)	Thol	24.20	4848	10.79	31528	1.84	19.37	405	8.66	229
13.	35 (K)	Chadasana	28.47	1193	10.45	45557	2.72	25.91	176	4.19	172
14.	52 (KL)	Rancharda	23.77	2066	9.33	25781	2.12	28.44	391	6.29	189
	Total (Mean)		25.60	3072	14.60	41785	2.92	28.47	321	6.48	212

APPENDIX IV—(Contd.)

TABLE (D) : **Composite table for selected villages**

Type of villages	Frequency	Mean per cent of irrigated land	Population 1981 Total	Growth rate 1971-81	Population potential 1981	Density (Hectare) 1981	per cent of non primary workers 1981	Amenities score 1981	Shops per 1000 population 1981	Development potential (1971-81)
High irrigation (>30 per cent)	15	53	3072	14.60	41728	2.92	28.47	321	6.48	212
Low irrigation (<18 per cent)	22	5	2363	28.49	34529	1.99	17.14	194	4.53	154

BIBLIOGRAPHY

Abler, R., J.S. Adams and P. Gould (1971), *Spatial Organisation : The Geographer's view of the World*, Prentice Hall, Englewood Cliffs, New Jersey.

Alam, Manzoor & Gopi, K.N. (Eds.) 1982, *Settlement Systems in India*, Oxford & IBH Pub. Co., New Delhi.

Baldev Singh, *Regional Planning Explorations in Agriculture and Industry*, Oxford & IBH Publishing Co.

Basu, D.N. and Raghu Roy and Pallavi Nikhil, *Impact of Agricultural Development on Demographic Behaviour*, Abhinav Publications, New Delhi.

Bhende, Asha A. and Kanitkar, Tara (1982), *Principles of Population Studies*, Himalaya Publishing House, Bombay-4.

Bhooshan, B.S. (Ed.) (1980), *Towards Alternative Settlement Strategies* (International Institute of Environment and Development), Heritage Pub., New Delhi.

Brady, Foust J. and Desouza, R. Anthony (1978), *The Economic Landscape—A Theoretical Introduction*, Charles E. Merrill Publishing Co., Ohio. 43216.

Chorley, R.J. and P. Haggett (1967), *Models in Geography*, Methuen, London.

Coffey, William (1981), *Geography—Towards a General Spacial Systems Approach*, Methuen-London, New York.

Chauhan, Brij Raj (1970), *Towns in the Tribal Setting*, National, Delhi.

Census (1951), *Mahesana District Census Handbook*, Government of Bombay, Director of Census Operations, Ahmedabad.

Census of Gujarat (1961), *District Census Handbook*, Mahesana District, Office of the Superintendent of Census Operations, Ahmedabad.

Census of India (1961), Volume V, Part VI-No. 5 Village Survey Monograph, Dist. Mahesana.

Census Part X-A & B (1971), *Town and Village Directory*, Village & Townwise Primary Census abstract.

Davidson Joan, Wibberley Gerald (1977), *Planning and the Rural Environment*, Pergamon International Library (Robert Maxwell), New York.

Deshpande, Arvind, Bapat S.B. (1980), *Indian Agriculture*, Jaico.

Geddes, Arthur (1982), *Man and Land in South Asia*, Concept Pub. Co., New Delhi.

Goodall, Brian and Kirby Andrew (1979), *Resources and Planning*, Pergamon International Library (Robert Maxwell) P.P. New York.

Government of Gujarat (1979), Report of the Gujarat State Land Commission, May, 1979.

Gupta, Halan, Desai (1982), *Development Planning and Policy*, Wiley Eastern Ltd., New Delhi.

Haggett, Peter (197), *Geography, A Modern Synthesis* (Series in Geography—D.W. Meining, Adviser), Harper and Row, New York.

Hancock, Tom (1976), *Growth Change in the Future City Region*, Leonard Hill.

Hofsten, L. Erland (1981), *Population : A comparative view of European and Indian Experience*, Hindustan Pub. Corp. Delhi.

Hotle, B.S. (Ed.) (1974), *Spatial Aspects of Development*, John Wiley & Sons, London.

Jaiswal, M.C. (1962), 'Inequality of Income distribution in India', in *Indian Economic Journal*, Vol. 9, No. 4.

Kumar, Pramila (1980), *Agricultural changes in Urban Fringe*, Rajesh Publications, New Delhi.

Laxminarayan, H. (1981), *Market Arrivals and Procurement of Wheat in Punjab and Haryana*, Agricole Publishing Academy, New Delhi.

Mabogunja, Akin L. (1980), *The Development Process—A* Spatial Perspective, Hutchinson University Library for Africa.

Mandal R.B. (1979), *Introduction to Rural Settlements*, Concept Pub. Co., New Delhi.

Mandal, R.B. and Peters G.L. (Eds.) (1982), *Urbanization and Regional Development*, Concept Pub. Co., New Delhi.

Mandal, R.B. (1981), *Planned Development of Rural Settlements*, Concept Pub. Co., New Delhi.

Maramis, J.B.P. (1980), *Local Level Planning and Rural Development*, Concept Pub. Co., New Delhi.

Mascarenhas, M.M. (1974), *Population Education for Life*, Oxford & IBH Pub. Co.

Michael, A.M. (1981), *Irrigation Theory and Practice*, Vikas Publishing House Pvt. Ltd.

Michael, Lipton (1980), *Why Poor People Stay Poor*, Urban Bias in World Development, Heritage Publishers, New Delhi.

Misra, R.P., Bhooshan, B.S. (1979), *Human Settlements in Asia* (Public Policies and Programmes), Heritage Publishers, New Delhi.

Mohammed, Noor (Ed.) (1981), *Perspectives in Agricultural Geography* (5 Vols.), Concept Pub. Co., New Delhi.

Nair, KRG (1982), *Regional Experience in a Developing Economy*, Wiley Eastern Ltd.

Nair, KRG (1981), *Regional Disparities in India*, Agricole Publishing Academy, New Delhi.

Nanjundappa, D.M. and Sinha, R.K. (1982), *Backward Area Development Problems & Prospects*, Sterling Publishers Pvt. Ltd.

Pacione, Michael (1981), *Problems and Planning in Third World Cities*, Vikas Publishing House Pvt. Ltd.

Pandey, M.P. (1979), *The Impact of Irrigation on Rural Development*, Concept Pub. Co., New Delhi.

Ramachandran, H. (1980), *Village Clusters and Rural Development*, Concept Pub. Co., New Delhi.

Rao, V.K.R.V. (1979), *Impact of Irrigation—Studies of Canal*, Well and Tank Irrigation in Karnataka.

Rao, V.M. (1980), *Rural Development and the Village Perspectives for Planning and Development*, Sterling Publishers Pvt. Ltd.

Sharma, A.N. (1981), *Spatial Approach for District Planning* (A Case Study of Karnal District), Concept Pub. Co., New Delhi.

Sharma, S.K., Malhotra, S.L. (1977), *Integrated Rural Development Approach, Strategy and Perspectives*, Abhinav Publications, New Delhi.

Singh, L.R. (Ed.) (1981), *New Perspectives in Geography*, (Thinker's Library), Allahabad, Prof. P. Dayal Felicitation Volume.

Sinha, M.M.P. (1980), *The impact of Urbanization on Land and use in the Rural-Urban Fringe*, Concept Pub. Co., New Delhi.

Stoodley, K.D.C. Lewis. T. Staintor, C.L.S. (1980), *Applied Statistical Techniques*, Ellis Horwood Limited, Chichester.

United Nations Development Programme (1976), Report No. DP/UN/IND-71-614/4, 'Ground Water Surveys in Rajasthan and Gujarat'.

Whyte, R.O. (1982), *The Spatial Geography of Rural Economics*, Oxford University Press.

Wrigly, N. and Bennett. R.J. (1981), *Quantitative Geography*, Routledge & Kegan Paul, London.

INDEX